A Venture Of Mind And Spirit

A VENTURE OF MIND AND SPIRIT

An Illustrated History of
Whitworth College

DALE E. SODEN

Dale E. Soden

Published by Whitworth College
Spokane, Washington

Printed in the U.S.A.
Ross Printing Company
Spokane, Washington

DEDICATION

Inevitably and appropriately,

this book is dedicated to the

students of Whitworth College,

past, present and future.

FOREWORD

rofessor Dale Soden has written this book as part of Whitworth College's centennial celebration. A centennial anniversary provides a college with the opportunity of focusing on its heritage.

During this centennial year, Whitworth College is giving thanks. Throughout his book, Dr. Soden points out the many hardships and struggles which the college experienced during much of its history. At the same time he identifies faculty members, administrators, trustees and friends of the college who responded by providing leadership and resources which helped Whitworth through difficult times. A current of gratitude runs through the book for the self-sacrifice, leadership, and commitment given to Whitworth by so many people.

That same gratitude is evident on campus during this centennial year. The names of noble forebears are being recited on numerous occasions; emeriti faculty, administrators, and staff members who are still living are the recipients of a variety of acts of gratitude. In this way, those of us who are currently working at the college are able to express our thanks for the institution which we currently enjoy.

During this centennial year we are bringing Whitworth's history to mind. We are re-acquainting ourselves with Whitworth's Christian identity and mission and renewing our dedication to the historic values of the college. The history of the college's values and traditions is like an aquifer running deep below the surface, upon which we draw for sustenance and enrichment. Beginning with the original purpose of the college — to educate both heart and mind — Professor Soden describes throughout the decades how the college sought to fulfill that purpose. Whitworth has attempted faithfully to be a certain kind of college, one that pursues both faith and learning while attempting to integrate these two themes in the lives of students. Soden's approach focuses upon the lives and activities of students. While it appears that students were frequently attempting to change the college, a careful reading shows that they appreciated the two-fold emphasis of the college and were intent on applying faith and learning to an ever-changing society. The history of Whitworth College is a story of faithfulness. Credit goes to the students, along with faculty members, administrators and trustees who have wrapped the college's historic values and purposes in contemporary expressions.

If the centennial celebration gives Whitworth an opportunity to look back, it also provides the opportunity to look ahead. One of the cardinal events of the centennial year was the ratification by the faculty and board of trustees of a new long-range plan. After having renewed its acquaintance with Whitworth's rich heritage, the entire college community engaged in a significant planning process. As president, I have challenged those of us at the college to remain true to our historic identity and mission, but at the same time to lift our sights, to have a larger vision of the role which Whitworth can play in American society. Building on a legacy that has integrated faith and learning, Whitworth College can become nationally known if we will bring a new level of excellence to our endeavors. America needs the kind of education which Whitworth offers. It is our obligation to pursue that level of excellence which will catch the nation's attention. This is Whitworth's challenge during the next quarter-century.

"The history of Whitworth College is a story of faithfulness."

Arthur De Jong
President
Whitworth College

Arthur J. De Jong
President, Whitworth College
February, 1990

PREFACE

A college's centennial anniversary provides a moment for reflecting on the founder's vision and on the people who have committed a good portion of their lives to the development of that vision. It is a moment to examine points of struggle and determination, and to remember decisions that have shaped the institution.

The course of history at Whitworth College has often been difficult. Moving from Sumner to Tacoma in 1899 and to Spokane in 1914, the college struggled to find a niche, while similar institutions in the Pacific Northwest failed. Despite financial woes and other problems, Whitworth's leaders persisted, believing that the nurturing of mind and spirit under the aegis of the Presbyterian Church was of utmost importance.

This book is not meant to be the definitive treatment of Whitworth College's rich past. It is intended, through words and images, to capture the essence of the Whitworth spirit and bring to light the contributions of many people who have played a role in its history. It is primarily intended to be a students' history, emphasizing activities and traditions of Whitworth students rather than details of presidential administrations or listings of faculty accomplishments. Nevertheless, I have tried to include influential faculty and to acknowledge important administrative leadership.

The book is organized chronologically. I understand that most alumni will turn first to their own era. I hope, however, that having done that, they will want to return to the beginning and read the work from cover to cover.

Inevitably, some people and their stories, some events and their significance are missing. For that I apologize. It would be impossible to complete a project of this nature and not be humbled by the number of people who have significantly contributed to the history of an institution. But limitations of space dictated the exclusion of a great deal of material. The decisions regarding what to include were difficult and, at times, painful.

As Whitworth heads into its second century, it is my fervent hope that those who currently serve at the college or attend as students will come to appreciate the work of those who have gone before. For 100 years, in the context of Christian love, dedicated people have committed themselves to a venture of mind and spirit, which has become our legacy. I trust that this same vision will continue to guide this college in the century to come.

The idea for this book grew out of conversations with several people including Jon Flora, Linda Sharman, and Joe Black. Special thanks are due to Linda Sharman who has patiently worked to make the text more readable. Her personal knowledge of Whitworth history has been invaluable and she suggested the title for the book. Don Woodward has lent his special talents toward the selection of photographs and has been responsible for the design and layout.

Additional thanks are due to Professor Lew Archer who not only read the text with a very careful eye but made many helpful suggestions. Terry Mitchell assisted in the editing in a significant way. Jennifer Jackson and John Carter have also made helpful contributions. Thanks are due Judi Puckett, Melissa Francis, and Amal Tanas for assistance in preparation of the manuscript.

My admiration for Professor Al Gray's work, *Not By Might*, written on the occasion of the 75th anniversary, is great. Not only is the book remarkably accurate, but it has been the source of a great deal of information in this work. Professor Gray's personal encouragement of this project as well as his help in reading the text and filling in gaps has been most valuable.

"Whitworth College confronts great opportunities; indeed Whitworth College is opportunity itself."

George F. Whitworth Founder Address to Synod, 1900

Whitworth owes a great deal to Al Gray for his work in helping recover a sense of the institution's past.

Other sources on the history of the college are very limited. The college archives contain a paper authored by Keith Murray ('35) on early Whitworth history. Dr. Murray later became a distinguished historian in his own right. Harry Soloos wrote one other paper which has provided helpful information regarding the Sumner and Tacoma period. Most of the material for this book came from the student newspaper, *The Whitworthian*, which goes back to 1905. Extensive use was also made of the college yearbook, *Natsihi*. Oral interviews with the following people provided valuable information: Hilda Bergman (the oldest living graduate of Whitworth, class of '09), Margaret Robertson, Burton Belknap, Grant Rodkey, Hazel Barnes, John Carlson, Mark Koehler, Alvin Quall, Nicolin Gray, Al Gray, Mike Goins, Ross Cutter, Laura Bloxham, Bob Clark, Walter Grosvenor, Paul Merkel, Jon Flora, Milton Johnson, Chuck Boppell, Betty Stratton, and Gail Fielding. Informal conversations with several other faculty members as well as current students provided other useful information.

The library staff, directed by Hans Bynagle, and including Bob Lacerte, Doris Banks, and Gail Fielding, has been most helpful. Bob Lacerte's organization of the photographic collection at Whitworth has made this project much easier.

Several people have donated photographs, including former president Mark Koehler, Ron Rice, Al Gray, Kathy Lee, and Jon Flora. Unless specifically mentioned, all other photographs are from the Whitworth College archives.

And finally I wish to express thanks to my colleagues on the faculty, administration, and support staff and specifically in the History/Political Studies Department for their encouragement. I give special thanks for my wife Peggy, and my two children, Joel and Marta, who have tolerated my unusual schedule with great love and patience. Without their support, this project would have not been possible.

Dale E. Soden

CONTENTS

CHAPTER I - 1890 -1899

GEORGE WHITWORTH'S VISION

The story of the first one hundred years of Whitworth College must begin with the life of George Whitworth. Most of us today would find the accomplishments of this pioneer Presbyterian pastor remarkable by any standard. But George Whitworth reflected much that ran deep in the nineteenth-century American character such as the virtue of democracy and the value of Christian higher education. He saw educational instruction as the essential key to spreading both the Gospel and American values. This vision marked the genesis of Whitworth College in the late nineteenth century. This vision still guides the administration and serves the faculty and students, one hundred years later.

Born on March 15, 1816, in Boston, England, George Whitworth came to the United States in 1828 with his parents, Matthew and Suzannah Whitworth, and his sister Emma. At age seventeen, George went to South Hanover College, Indiana, where he later graduated. When he was twenty-two, George married Mary Elizabeth Thomson from Louisville, Kentucky. She came from a

Above Right - Earliest portrait: George Whitworth as a young lawyer in Greensburg, Indiana (circa 1840)

Above Left - George Whitworth: Missionary, farmer, businessman and president of the University of Washington

Below Left - Whitworth College: "In the shadow of Mount Rainier"

Facing Page - Three founders: (l to r) Whitworth, Amos T. Fox (1890), 2nd president Calvin Stewart (1890-1898)

long line of Presbyterian ministers and missionaries.

During the next fifteen years he was both a high school principal in Lancaster, Ohio, and a lawyer in Greensburg, Indiana, and Dayton, Ohio. In 1844, Whitworth began study at the New Al-

Above - The whole college: Students, faculty and administrators at Sumner

Right - Reverend George Whitworth in Seattle at age 88

bany (Indiana) Theological Seminary. Ordained in 1848 by the New Albany Presbytery, he served churches in Corydon and Cannelton, Indiana and Hawesville, Kentucky. Still, he was restless. Whitworth turned his eyes to the far West. In April 1852, he wrote of his intentions:

"It is intended that we shall, as soon as possible after settlement, establish a good parochial school for the benefit of the children and youth of the colony, to be suited to their immediate wants; and no efforts will be spared to elevate the character of the school, and to make it an institution of learning of the highest grade, so soon as the interests of the colony may demand it. It should be a settled principle, that no child or youth, connected with the colony, shall ever be permitted to grow up without the benefit of a good English education, and a thorough religious training."

A year after his appointment in 1852 to be a missionary to Puget Sound, Whitworth had organized fifteen families to head west from St. Louis. But by the time they set forth for the Pacific Northwest, the party had dwindled to the Whitworths and two other families. The intrepid band eventually linked up with two other families, bringing the total party to thirty-five — twenty-five women and ten men.

Although the party avoided complete disaster, disease ravaged the cattle, and the families began to separate and seek different destinations. The group temporarily abandoned the idea of establishing a Presbyterian colony in the Pacific Northwest and only the Whitworths took a steamer down the Columbia River to Portland in October 1853.

Undaunted, Whitworth soon helped establish the First Presbyterian Church in Portland. When spring came, however, the Puget Sound country, with its great inland waterway, drew him on. At present-day Olympia, he conducted the first Presbyterian service in the territory north of the Columbia River.

From the beginning, Whitworth significantly influenced the educational and religious life of the Pacific Northwest. Besides Portland and Olympia, he started churches at Grand Mound and Claquato, where Chehalis now stands.

During the Indian War of 1855-56, Whitworth traveled with a gun on his shoulder to preach to these churches. Shortly thereafter, Whitworth began another church on Whidbey Island near Coupeville, and finally, in 1869, he established the First Presbyterian Church in Seattle. In all, sources credit Whitworth with organizing as many as twenty churches.

Whitworth also became deeply involved in the life of Washington Territory as a farmer, lawyer, businessman, and as chief clerk of the Indian Department of Washington Territory. Whitworth, the entrepreneur, helped develop coal fields east of Lake Washington.

Through it all, his interest in education never flagged. He served both Thurston and King Counties as superintendent of schools. Whitworth was largely responsible for drafting the organic educational law of Washington Territory. His greatest renown, however, came as the president of the young University of Washington, first from 1866 to 1867 until it closed due to a shortage of funds, and then from 1874 to 1876. But his dream of founding a Presbyterian institution continued to drive him. He continued to look for opportunities to fulfill his vision — a higher education institution in the Pacific Northwest that would integrate faith and learning.

Above - *The Sumner building*

Right - *President Calvin Stewart*

THE ACADEMY YEARS

Conditions for education in the region were anything but favorable during the 1860s and 1870s. Too little money and too few students were available. But by the beginning of the 1880s, prospects improved slightly and Whitworth thought perhaps it would be now or never for his dream of a Presbyterian colony and academy. In 1880, he registered the organization with the territorial capital. Everywhere he went, he spoke about the need for an educational institution for Presbyterians.

The site he selected was Sumner. Set in the Puyallup Valley with a beautiful vista of Mt. Rainier, it seemed an excellent choice.

On January 7, 1884, the academy opened in the Sumner Presbyterian Church with its pastor, the Rev. George A. McKinlay, as principal. Students sat at desks built on the backs of pews.

Despite a crop failure in the Puyallup Valley, Whitworth immediately launched a building campaign for the academy. By spring of 1885, the first floor of a new building was completed, largely funded by a $4,000.00 loan from L.F.

Thompson, the valley's leading hops grower and vice-president of the board of trustees. For the next five years, Whitworth and the trustees scratched for money. Finally, in 1889, the building was completed. The first floor housed a chapel that could seat 125 students, as well as living quarters for the faculty. The first floor also included a dining room, kitchen, music rooms, and the library.

Above - The first Whitworth graduate: Calvin Stewart, son of the president

The second floor contained rooms for female students and the dean of women, as well as two rooms for recitations.

WHITWORTH COLLEGE

On February 19, 1890, the eight incorporators of Sumner Academy voted to change the name of the institution to Whitworth College. According to Alfred O. Gray, historian of the college, the move was spurred by competition from public high schools and also because several Presbyterian ministers, including Whitworth, simply wanted to create a college. On February 20, the trustees signed the "Articles of Incorporation of the Whitworth College of Sumner," and elected the Rev. Amos T. Fox, principal of the academy, as president. Shortly thereafter, Fox's father-in-law, the Reverend Calvin W. Stewart, came to Sumner and relieved Fox as president.

The faculty and administration modeled the early curriculum on that of Eastern colleges. The first catalogue declared that the college was committed to "guarding well the moral and religious life of the students, ever directing them in the pursuit of that learning and culture of heart and mind that make the finished scholar." This emphasis on both heart and mind would serve as Whitworth's guiding vision for the next century. From the outset, faculty and administrators agreed that the integration of faith and intellect would be their primary challenge.

The first two degrees were baccalaureates in the classical department and the scientific department. The college also offered courses in music, art, and commercial subjects. There was a preparatory department and a normal department to allow teachers to prepare for public schools. By 1891, there was a department of elocution and a "Ladies Course," which eliminated Greek "to give

Sumner Academy,

Under the care of the Presbytery of Puget Sound.

A Boarding and Day School for the Youth of both Sexes.

————✛✛————

This Academy is at the village of Sumner, W. T., a station on the railroad leading from Tacoma to Seattle, and is about twelve miles from Tacoma.

The situation is healthy, and the moral surroundings are all that parents could desire. No saloons, or places for sale of intoxicating drinks are allowed, these being excluded by provision made, as part of the consideration in every deed for town lot

The Academy is in its second year, with increased facilities and brightening prospects. The new building is expected to be ready by the opening of the next term, which begins on

Monday, Jan. 5, 1885; ends March 27, 1885

The Academy is in charge of REV. GEO. A. McKINLAY, assisted by competent and experienced teachers.

TERMS:

Board, Room Rent and Washing, per week,	$5.00

TUITION

Primary Class, per Term,	$ 6.00
Intermediate Studies, per Term,	8.00
Higher English, including Languages and Book-keeping, per Term,	10.00
Instrumental Music, twenty-four lessons,	15.00
Painting in Oil,	12.00

For further particulars address the Principal,

REV. GEO. A. McKINLAY,
Sumner, Pierce Co., W. T.

the ladies more time for the study of music and art and other accomplishments." Courses such as "Railroad Curves" engaged students of civil engineering. The college required business students to take courses in Egyptian history, elocution, and astronomy.

Life on the Sumner campus, like that at other church-related college campuses in the 1890s, meant strict supervision of student activity, particularly when it involved even the possibility of contact with the opposite sex. The catalogues in the Sumner years contained the "Abstract Rules of Government," which provide a flavor of Victorian America transplanted in the Pacific Northwest.

1. Students are responsible for the order of their rooms.
2. Students absent from any class without excuse are not entitled to recite until excused.
3. Persons calling upon young ladies must present letters of introduction from parents or guardians.
4. Visitors are not admitted to the private apartments of young ladies. Calls are not allowed to interfere with study hours. No calls permitted on the Sabbath.
5. The young ladies boarding in the school will not visit the town without permission.

Students attended a compulsory chapel service, and college regulations mandated that each student attend church on Sunday. Students reported on Monday where they had worshipped on the previous day. The college required attendance at a Presbyterian Church only in cases where a student expressed no preference.

Students who violated the above-mentioned rules risked receiving a demerit, or being reprimanded, suspended, or expelled, according to the nature of the offense.

College administrators and faculty assured parents that while men and women occupied separate wings of the same building, under no circumstances would access be permitted from one side to the other. All students were required to have permission in order to leave the campus. The sight of the dean of women, Miss Edmiston, chaperoning female students as they walked on country roads or attended church became familiar to Sumner residents.

In those early days, students lived primarily in the surrounding hills of the Puyallup Valley and present-day Orting. Most travelled on horseback, although some came by train. Harry Soloos, an early writer of Whitworth history, told of a student who rode a buckboard to town each morning to attend classes after selling cream and butter from the family farm.

As was common with other colleges, Whitworth expected its students to participate in literary societies and attend religious and musical events. Whitworth, in its earliest years, sponsored the Calliopean and Lowell Literary Societies with an annual contest in which students read their literary efforts. According to Gray, "Some alumni later admitted that their presence at these affairs was not due to any literary inclination but to the excellent opportunities afforded to walk some young lady home."

Pranks were common, as students sometimes chafed under the supervision. One Halloween, the male students strung a wire from the college building to a student's home across the street and hung crockery used for toilet purposes on the wire--there was no indoor plumbing. Spotting the line-up next morning, Professor Fox took out his rifle (a reminder that Sumner was still the "Old West"), and shot down the so-called "white owls," much to the students' amusement.

Facing Page, Above Left - Early Sumner Academy advertising

Facing Page, Lower Left - Tennis Courts on the Sumner Campus

Facing Page, Above Right - 1893 Students: James L. Stewart, Frank Blackburn, Albert C. Stewart, Fred Whitworth, James Hill

Above - Down by the tracks: Students headed to a Tacoma athletic contest

Above - *Interior decorators: Students at Sumner*

Right - *Track stars: Jim Hill and Fred Long display their medals*

According to one account, the handles hung on the wire for months. On other occasions, students stole outhouses from their rightful owners and used them to block Main Street. One group of young men disassembled some wagons and reassembled them atop several Sumner buildings.

Students felt an intense pride in their newly established institution and gathered regularly to support their peers at sporting events. By 1893, Whitworth won its first Washington Intercollegiate Athletic Association track title. Whitworth's teams won the WIAA championship for four more years, defeating teams from the University of Washington, University of Puget Sound, Washington College, Tacoma Academy, and Vashon University. Students played baseball as early as 1893 and football as early as 1895.

While there was much to cheer about during the 1890s, Whitworth was plagued by financial crises and erratic enrollments. In 1890-91, only seventy-eight students attended during one of

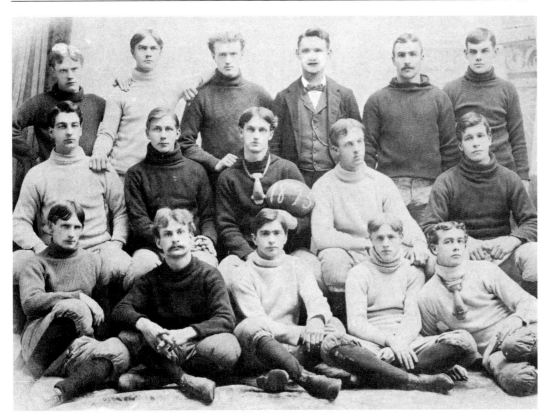

the three terms, although probably no more than 15 were college students.

When the price of hops fell from $1.40 to only five cents a bushel between 1892 and 1893, the ability of the local economy to support Whitworth virtually disappeared overnight. Enrollment dropped from ninety-one to fifty-six; Fox and Stewart scoured the back-country looking for prospective students, often accepting dairy products and food staples for tuition. Faculty and administration often sacrificed their entire salaries to keep the institution afloat. Repeatedly, George Whitworth, as head of the trustees, extended his own financial resources and saved the college.

During the early days, college administrators constantly wrestled with the issue of location. Sumner was simply too remote from the growing population centers on Puget Sound. Offers began to come in from Seattle, Tacoma, and Port Townsend. In 1893, a serious offer of land in West Seattle was initially accepted with the idea that the name would change to "The University of the Pacific Northwest." The offer, contingent on the college raising more money to build new buildings, had to be declined. In 1897, another offer, the Eisenbis Hotel in Port Townsend, was accepted but later rejected by the Presbyterian Board of Aid.

Stewart resigned as president that same year, but agreed to remain as a principal fund raiser. The Reverend Robert Boyd succeeded Stewart, but it was Stewart who convinced H. O. Armour, brother of Philip D. Armour of the Armour Packing Company, to donate $50,000 to Whitworth, then the largest gift to a denominational college on the West Coast.

It became clear that the college's future success depended on being more accessible to students. As a result, the trustees looked increasingly to Tacoma.

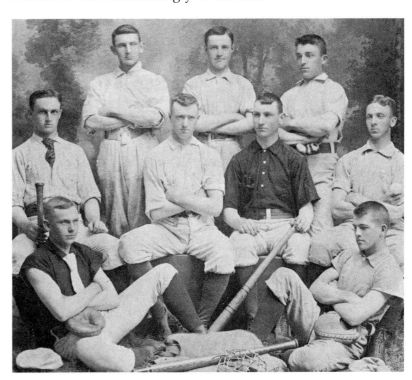

Chapter II 1899 -1914

The Tacoma Years

*I*n 1880, when George Whitworth first looked for a site for his educational institution, Tacoma was not much different from Sumner. Few streets existed and its 1,098 people went about their daily lives in dust and mud. But by 1888, Tacoma was booming. Population numbered nearly 35,000; buildings had sprung up overnight with graded streets and "modern" utilities. After Tacoma was named the Northern Pacific Railroad's western terminus, circulars of the era called it "the place where rail and sail meet at Commencement Bay."

In the mid '90s, Tacoma looked more and more attractive as a site at which to relocate the college. The Depression of 1893, which had jeopardized Whitworth's existence in Sumner, played an important role in the decision to move to Tacoma. Tacoma real estate developer Allen C. Mason owned an enormous mansion on Tacoma's Inspiration Point and had arranged to bring the streetcar line near it. But with the depression, financial difficulties forced Mason to sell.

In July 1899, Whitworth trustees reached an agreement to buy the Mason estate — the large residence and grounds — for $22,000. Eventually the campus expanded to nearly 14 acres.

As an early catalogue describes, the view from the new campus was spectacular: "From its spacious colonnade and verandas a most beautiful, inspiring, picturesque landscape, sea and mountain scene can be had. In front stretches the

opposite wooded shoreline, which rises upward to the foothills of the Cascade range, flanked on the north by Mt. Baker and toward the south by St. Helens, nearly the scope of the State; while the magnificent father of the mountains, snow-crowned, touched with silvery splendor by the sun, looms up seventy miles to the east, superb, grand in unchallenged stateliness. To the left the eye reaches as far as it can see down the peaceful waters of Puget Sound in the direction of Seattle, dotted here and there with huge white steamers and ocean freighters moving hither and thither like gigantic swans casting their shadows upon the waters."

Transportation to campus in the Tacoma years was an adventure; some students came by boat to the wharves,

Facing Page - The Collonade on Ladies' Hall

Above - Tacoma and Mt. Rainier from campus: "A most beautiful, inspiring, picturesque landscape"

Below - Ladies' Hall and the Sound: "A location unexcelled in America"

ties of an urban world.

Franklin Gault, who became president of the college in 1899, was the first president to be a layman and the first to hold a doctoral degree. A school superintendent in the 1880s, he had been named the first president of the University of Idaho in 1892.

The college lacked adequate enrollment to hold classes during the fall of 1899 but resumed in January 1900, with President Gault, three faculty members, and fifteen students. Enrollment in Tacoma peaked in 1907-09 with 83 college students and 230 overall.

Nevertheless, Whitworth's financial woes continued. A $200,000 endowment campaign, launched in 1903, fell far short. H. O. Armour gave a total of $100,000, but that money was rapidly expended.

But there was growth, too. In 1902, Mrs. W. A. Olmstead gave Whitworth an 11-room residence, Olmstead Hall. In 1904, Mr. and Mrs. S. W. Erwin gave $6,000 for the construction of Erwin Hall, which contained science and physical culture classrooms, music facilities, and the women's dormitory. The city of Tacoma donated to the college the Mason Library, with 6,000 volumes, stipulating

then disembarked to catch the Pacific Avenue trolley line. Others arrived by train, caught the Pacific Avenue car line in front of the depot, got off at Ninth and Pacific and walked two blocks uphill to where the Point Defiance cars left every ten minutes. The ride took them to North 43rd, two blocks from the college. Whitworth students were learning the reali-

that the library be open to the public two days a week. The library building included a chapel that seated 400. Of the buildings which comprised the Whitworth campus in Tacoma, only the gymnasium remains.

Gault worked energetically to build a first-rate residential campus dedicated to the liberal arts. He wanted to eliminate the practical arts that had marked the curriculum in the Sumner years. He also did not want the college to evolve into a Bible school. The 1902-03 catalogue reflected Gault's concern about the liberal arts: "It must be kept in mind all the time that knowledge is not the highest value sought, but culture, the discipline of the powers, the vitalizing of the faculties and the developing of self-activity. Broad contact, expanded point of view, the ability to look over enlarged vistas, to make men and women broad without making them shallow — that is our ideal of culture . . . . More briefly, Whitworth College gives the humanities first place among studies, insists upon the supreme value of mental discipline, and seeks to promote the

ideals of life."

The 1902 curriculum included 110 courses in 13 academic areas; ancient languages comprised approximately one-fourth of the courses. Ten courses in science were divided among biology, chemistry, and physics. The other fields included philosophy, German, French, English, history, mathematics, and Bible. The college held both preparatory classes and college degree courses.

Above - Beautiful carved fireplace in the parlor of the Ladies' Hall

Below - The 1907-08 student body poses in front of Ladies' Hall (Mason Mansion)

Top - *Mason Hall library and classrooms*

Center Left - *Men's Hall and campus buildings*

Center Right - *Olmsted Hall: Housing for missionaries' children while at college*

Bottom - *An interior view : The Mason Hall library*

The 1906 catalogue cited these reasons to attend Whitworth:

"It stands for the highest type of American citizenship.

It has an ideal location, pure, healthful environment.

It has an unsurpassed curriculum in Classical, Philosophical, and Scientific Courses, Music, Art, Public Expression, Commercial.

You can get what you need.

It stands pre-eminent in college life, and scholastic attainment. Whitworth is first class, high grade.

It seeks to impart Eastern Atlantic culture and refinement and democratic spirit."

Perhaps it was Gault's vision that led to the college being awarded a Rhodes Scholarship in 1908. During the early twentieth century, the scholarships were awarded to institutions. Faculties would select the appointee, who received $1500 per year for three years. Using an examination provided by Oxford, the Whitworth faculty found two Whitworth students qualified: Frederic D. Metzger and Kenneth Ghormley. Metzger won the final election by a very slim margin.

Metzger was not only an outstanding student but a great athlete; he also served as manager of the minstrel show, one of the largest social events of the year, and worked as editor of the newspaper. Ghormley was equally well-rounded and involved in the life of the

college.

While the Board of Trustees stressed academics, members also consciously assured parents of properly supervised residential life. The 1904 catalogue emphasized that "all harmful amusements, such as dancing and card playing, are strictly forbidden in the college, and on the part of the pupils committed to our custody."

The staff made great efforts to create what was affectionately known as "home life" on campus. Publications emphasized values such as kindness, thoughtfulness, courtesy, order, right, and good will. A sense of decorum prevailed in that "no one [should] be admitted to the college family circle who is unworthy of confidence and respect. For this reason no applicant is received as a boarder who is not well-recommended

Above - The Gymnasium and Literary Hall

Below - Rhodes Scholars: Kenneth Ghormley (r) qualified, but only Frederic Metzger (l) went to Oxford

This Page - *A student boating expedition on Puget Sound*

by persons known to the college authorities as entirely responsible. The sole condition is moral worth, not birth, position or wealth."

The Whitworthian, during the Tacoma years, reveals an appealing campus life — dynamic, intellectual, and just plain fun.

School traditions flourished, partly because students were less mobile before the age of the automobile and partly because the college's size allowed students to share leadership of everything from social events and literary activities to athletics, dramatics, journalism, and debate.

Sophomores regularly dictated to the freshmen what they could and could not do. For example, in 1908 the sophomores printed a "Manifesto" which

spelled out certain conditions for behavior:

1) Freshmen must consider themselves as valets to noble sophomores and be ready when called upon to black their shoes, brush their clothes, and assist in any way possible their superiors.

2) Freshmen residents of the clubhouse must sweep and scrub the halls and porches, keep the lawn in good condition, carry water, coal and wood, answer phone calls and attend to other duties as they may arise.

3) Freshmen must never bow before the giant nicotine or perform the rights of Bacchus on the Whitworth campus in the city of Destiny, or in the county of Pierce.

4) A Freshman must tip his hat to all sophomores, and when passing a sopho-

Left - *A Whitworth tradition: Campus Day clean up*

Below - *Self-portrait: Students with a Brownie camera*

more girl must step off the sidewalk, holding his hat over the left shoulder and having his eyes look towards the ground, and remain stationary until she has passed.

5) Freshmen must not indulge in the rights of their superiors--that is, using stiff hats, dress-suits, canes, fancy hat bands, patent leather shoes, colored pocket-handkerchiefs, etc...But they shall dress in plain, neat, Buster Brown suits of green color, with large white collars.

One early Whitworth tradition, the "Cane Rush," helped determine class supremacy. Earlier, freshman and sophomore classes engaged in free-for-alls that ended in "broken heads and furniture — and which settled nothing." By 1908, the melee had developed only slightly more organization. "At 3:15 the two classes lined up — the Freshmen ten strong, while the Sophs could muster but seven. Coach Rueber tossed the cane into the air, and then for the next ten minutes followed a melee, which for being 'intense' and 'strenuous' beat a football scrimmage all to pieces. At the end of that time the contestants were dragged apart one by one, and it was found that the Freshmen had eight hands on the cane, while the Sophs had but four." — February, 1908 *Whitworthian*

The minstrel show, with its racial implications, has fallen from favor, but it served as a major form of entertainment

early in the century at Whitworth and at other colleges. In February 1905, *The Whitworthian* recounted how Professor Schutz spent hours working with students to perfect their routines. "Whitworth's leading young men with blackened faces and grotesque attire in the midst of beautiful stage settings...were liberally remembered by their friends in the audience... with choice bouquets of alfalfa, turnips, beets, and other vegetables."

In those early years, the college did not allow men into female rooms, but the students still found ways of meeting the opposite sex through events such as residence hall tours. One such tour had a railroad theme. "On entrance in the reception hall the monstrous sign of 'Waiting Room' met the gaze. Here was found the Depot Matron anxious to help you, and

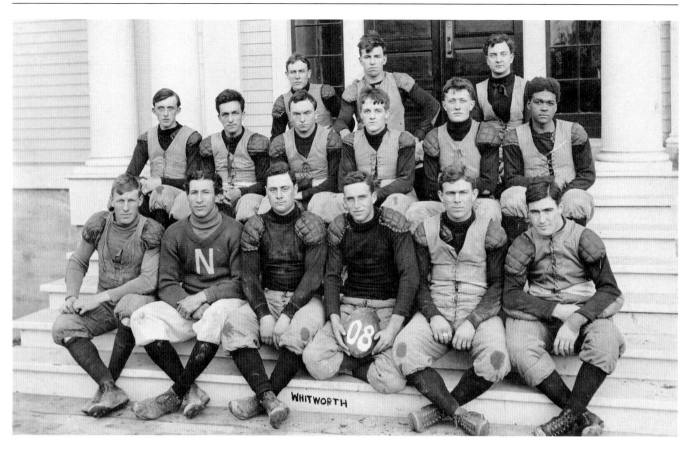

the Ticket Agent, indeed amiable, as she made out your ticket as to name and time of departure. Through all the journey mapped out obstacles loomed up at every turn as you went from room to room. The object of the game was to make the complete round of the rooms in the shortest time." — March, 1906 *Whitworthian*

Another tradition, the football banquet, involved elaborate preparations by the ladies of the faculty and the Students' Association. They decorated a hall with flowers and college colors for a night of speeches and the singing of college songs such as:

Where is it you should turn your step
When seeking college work or prep?
The school that has the daisy red,

'Tis Whitworth; oh 'tis Whitworth
Where is the brainiest faculty
The wisest bunch you'll see
Who'll make you what you ought to be?
At Whitworth; oh at Whitworth
Where are the boys of brain and brawn,
The girls whose charms have wide renown,
Whose spirits high shall ne'er go down?
At Whitworth, oh at Whitworth
What college has us most impressed,
And just because it is the best
Of all the schools in East or West?
'Tis Whitworth; oh 'tis Whitworth.

— March, 1908 Whitworthian

You can talk about your Cambridge
And your Princeton and Cornell
You may preach about old Oxford
And Johns Hopkins just as well
But my friend, I'm here to tell you
That these schools must all go back
And get down in supplication
To the Crimson and the Black
Chorus:
Drink her down for good old Whitworth;
For the school you can't keep back;
fill it up to overflowing
For the Crimson and the Black
Here is where you find the athletes;
Here is where the brain will grow;
Here is where the soul develops
And all 'round we're not so slow

Left - Baseball: The
boys of summer
attracted big crowds

Below - Tug-of-War:
Freshman-sophomore
competition

Teachers with the best of training
We may truly boast of here,
And they work for all that's in them
To advance their pupils dear.
Chorus:

— *March, 1908 Whitworthian*

High above Puget's water
Grand old Whitworth lifts her head,
Our stately Alma Mater
Of whom shall e'er be said
Her leal sons and daughters
Her praises sing forever,
Prosperity be hers
Forever and for aye
Here's to our college,
Whitworth, forever more.

— *February, 1910 Whitworthian*

The football game, besides being an outlet for school spirit, was also an important social event as reflected in the following from a 1908 *Whitworthian:*

"After the Willamette game Saturday, November 21, the Whitworth girls entertained in the Residence in honor of the Whitworth and Willamette elevens. . . .Later in the evening an informal program was given, consisting of selections by the orchestra, vocal group by Miss Dykeman, and piano solos by Miss Robinson and Miss Rolleston. After dainty refreshments were served by the Misses

Bernice George, Russell, Presby and Brown, the Willamette boys left to catch their train, saying that they didn't mind being beaten by Whitworth at all, after the jolly time we had given them."

The 1908 football team won games over University of Oregon and Whitman College, but the big game was against University of Washington. Years later, legendary Husky Coach Gil Dobie recalled that game. "I doubt if ever I shall feel as well-satisfied as I did when my men trotted off the field with a 24 to 4 score in their favor....For 40 minutes of that game...Whitworth was playing us off our feet and just missed scoring touchdowns several times. But [Coach Arthur] Rueber had coached his team to play only 40 minutes. I insisted on a longer second half and in the last 10 minutes, Washington made all its points and won the game."

Periodically, editorials about the

Above - Galloping ghosts: Football scrimmage at Tacoma

Below - Rev. Barend Kroeze, 5th president (1905-1909)

Facing Page Bottom - The Troubadors: Dormitory friends from 1905

role of athletics at a Christian college raised issues about injuries and whether football should be permitted. But in general, support remained strong for athletics, as indicated in one early school bulletin. "The chief problem is to keep the sports from degenerating into brutal combats, contests of beef strength to 'see who can do the other fellow.' There is little danger of this tendency being accentuated in the manly sports at Whitworth where the environment and training and control make for Christian culture, gentlemanly graces, courtesy, respect, honesty, nobility and high scholarship. Football, tennis, baseball and track work are avocations, not vocations of students; essentials to the development of the best manhood."

Baseball also proved to be very popular with Whitworth students. "The State University has the advantage of almost unlimited material from which to pick, while Whitworth has only about twenty men from which it may select a team," the April, 1905 *Whitworthian* noted, adding that while the University of Washington won 4-0, three runs were scored in the ninth on "some slow fielding and a lucky three-bagger." The college team took trips to eastern Washington and played teams in Prosser and Ritzville as well as Gonzaga College, Spokane High School, and the Blair Business College.

The student body provided all of the funding for college sports. A report from the treasurer of the Student Association in 1909 lists bills for such things as clay

for the baseball diamond ($8.00); an advertisement in the *Tacoma Tribune* ($2.40); baseballs ($15.00); and a hospital bill for a student injured during one of the games ($22.50).

Along with its spirit of fun, the Tacoma period produced a number of remarkable graduates, including: Lillian G. Stevenson, M.D., first Whitworth graduate to become a physician; John W. Crandall, a noted New York maritime lawyer and prominent soloist; Dosu Doseff, M.D., Chicago physician; William John McCauley, M.D.; Kenneth I. Ghormley, Rhodes Scholar qualifier and Seattle attorney; Ruth Dunbar, journalist and author of *The Lafayette Escadrille*; Frederic D. Metzger, Tacoma attorney and Whitworth's first Rhodes Scholar; George Rossman, Associate Justice of the Supreme Court of Oregon; David J. Guy, hydraulics engineer for the U.S. Chamber of Commerce; William L. Paul, Alaskan attorney and legislator and later a Seattle attorney; Monroe G. Everett, president of Trinity University; Joseph Turner, M.D., well-known for an important blood discovery; David H. Johnson, M.D., Tacoma's famous "Baby Doctor" with 8,300 deliveries to his credit; Ralph Ghormley, M.D., orthopedic surgeon at the Mayo Clinic and internationally known physician; and Miss Bertha Lee, administrator with *Reader's Digest*.

President Gault resigned in 1905 to take the presidency of the University of South Dakota. The Reverend Barend H. Kroeze, the former dean of Lennox College, succeeded him in August 1905. Fund raising appeared to be Kroeze's strength; he secured a pledge from Andrew Carnegie for $25,000 and ceased drawing from the Armour fund. Enrollment reached its highest level under his administration with 235 total students; this was not to be achieved again until 1934-35.

Kroeze was not particularly popular with the students, perhaps because he was off campus much of the time. Students signed petitions indicating that they preferred that the college be turned over to Dean Donald MacKay, and on one occasion they burned Kroeze in effigy.

Kroeze also found himself at odds with perhaps the most powerful trustee in Whitworth history, the Reverend Mark A. Matthews, pastor of Seattle's First Presbyterian Church. By 1908, Matthews' church was the largest Presbyterian church in the United States with close to 9,000 members. He participated actively in Seattle politics and became increasingly involved in the hiring and firing of Whitworth faculty and administration. Kroeze objected and submitted his resignation. The Board refused to accept it, but nevertheless turned over the internal administration to MacKay. Kroeze tried to resign on two more occasions and, finally, in August 1909, the Board accepted his decision.

For two years the Board searched for a president, only to come back to Dean MacKay who assumed the position on September 1, 1911. The difficulty in securing a president may be partly attributable to the ongoing financial difficulties. The records show criticism of the Synod for a lack of support during these years. The city of Tacoma also showed little interest and the Col-

lege of Puget Sound and Pacific Lutheran Academy represented major competition for Tacoma's support. Thus, the trustees again began to look elsewhere for a college site.

Top - *Dean of the Faculty Albert Heath (l) and Literature Professor Liberta Brown (r)*

Above - *Japanese students at Whitworth*

Chapter III - 1914 - 1920

The Move To Spokane

In 1890, as Whitworth College was emerging from its Sumner Academy beginnings, the way was already being prepared for its final destination in Spokane. Spokane realtor and mining mogul Jay P. Graves wanted to attract a college to his city and invested in a tract northwest of Spokane in hopes of luring Washington State Agricultural College to the site. Fortunately for Whitworth, Graves' bid was unsuccessful. But Graves did not abandon the idea as he continued to build his Country Homes Development Company.

About 1912, Spokane Presbyterians began voicing a need for a Presbyterian college in the region. Two Whitworth trustees, the Reverend Hugh H. McMillan and J. Grier Long, were members of the Spokane Presbytery. So, in the fall of 1913, a region's desire for a college and a college's need for a location converged and Graves' offer of land welded them together.

Graves agreed to allocate 640 acres for the college. Forty acres would serve as the campus and 40 acres would be put up for immediate sale to establish a building fund. The remaining acreage was to be

platted and sold with 45 to 55 per cent of the proceeds going to the college. An official of the College Board of Aid called the offer exceptionally generous, and called Spokane "the best city in the country in which to establish a college."

The Whitworth board agreed to move the college if a $100,000 building fund could be raised. If the Spokane community raised $70,000, the Synod of Washington pledged to provide the remaining $30,000.

Spokane citizens launched the campaign with great enthusiasm and rivalry among 10 teams, nine groups of men and one of women. The leader of the latter group was quoted in the *Spokesman-Review* of January 25, 1914.

"Why, we have $20,000 in

Left - Groundbreaking for McMillan Hall on May 22, 1914

Below - Attention!: World War I era lineup in front of McMillan Hall

Facing Page - President Donald MacKay (1911-1917) guided transition from Tacoma to Spokane

Above - *Jay P. Graves:*
He gave Whitworth
640 acres in 1914

Top - *Aerial view of*
Ballard and McMillan
Halls

Below - *Gothic*
dreams: Plans for
Whitworth's eventual
growth

Facing Page Top -
"Alas, poor Yorick":
Professor Holcombe's
biology class in base-
ment of Men's Dorm

Facing Page, Center -
David Guy: Versatile
professor, surveyor,
dean, and tenor "who
coached all athletics,
managed all teams"

sight right now," said Mrs. A. H. Verrall. "We did little today because of getting our work organized, and because to most of us women Saturday morning means baking for the coming week. But starting Monday we will get after that $20,000, which we have set as a mark for our team, even if our husbands do have to go out and visit a bakery or a downtown restaurant."

The campaign was a success, and on May 22, 1914, the Reverend Conrad Bluhm, pastor of the Centenary Presbyterian Church and president of the Spokane Ministerial Association, broke ground for the college. "This shovel, with which we render the joyous task," said Bluhm, "is neither irreligious nor sectarian. It is broadly evangelical." Shortly thereafter, construction began on a $30,000 dormitory and administration building, and by

mid-summer, building commenced on a second dormitory which later became Ballard Hall after Captain W. C. Ballard of Seattle, who served as a trustee from 1892-1927.

Two hundred people attended the dedication of the first building, the Young Ladies' Dormitory, on August 26, 1914. Speeches, documents in the cornerstone, and a blessing of corn, wine, oil, and water marked the ceremony in the middle of the campus stand of pine trees. In 1924, the name was changed to McMillan Hall in honor of Trustee Hugh McMillan.

On September 23, 1914, classes began, and on October 14, the second dormitory building was dedicated. Enrollment numbered forty students of college rank along with seven preparatory and five unclassified students.

The faculty numbered 14, of whom

four had come with President MacKay from Tacoma.

By January 1915, the college had spent nearly $60,000 on two dormitories, classroom equipment, an athletic field, tennis courts, a water system and a gas plant. They added a temporary gymnasium, the President's home (now MacKay Hall), and two faculty homes during 1915. Tremendous enthusiasm gripped the board and the student body. In June 1915, the board unveiled a plan for the campus which included eighteen brick buildings, a large chapel in the center, and a football stadium.

For most of the early years of the college, Whitworth required faculty to be exceptionally versatile and often to teach outside their disciplines. But few professors have had careers as varied as that of David J. Guy, a Tacoma alumnus. One of the four professors who came with Dr. MacKay from Tacoma, Guy taught mathematics and civil engineering, and also was the athletic director. He is remembered as the one "who coached all athletics, managed all teams and served as math instructor, campus surveyor, dean of men, dormitory head, second tenor in the quartet, and adviser of his male fussers."

Below - The campus in 1915

Above - *A studious
scene in the Men's
Lounge*

Below - *Good music,
books and conversation:
Women's Lounge in
McMillan Hall*

Faculty members maintained more formal relationships during the early twentieth century and demanded more deference from students than in recent years. Yet, paradoxically, those early Whitworth students seemed to experience a deep sense of intimacy with their professors; humor, the universal bonding agent, helped cement students to faculty in a profound way.

The 1915 *Natsihi* revealed the following about Whitworth faculty: "Strange as it may seem, there is sometimes an advantage in being looked down upon: in chapel, for instance, the students by virtue of their positions get such a splendid view of the faculty. Dr. MacKay occupies the middle of the faculty stage. Rising suddenly, with head erect, chest out, he marches to the edge of the platform, halts, strikes a Napoleonic attitude and in the tones of Patrick Henry announces the hymn. After the singing he abruptly turns his back on the audience, marches back to his chair, adjusts his coattails and sits down. Professor Guy usually wears white socks. With his hands shoved deep into his pockets, his lips slightly compressed, his eyes wandering indifferently about the room, he makes a picture that the students would be loath to forget. Dr. Hollingsworth sits bolt upright, both feet firmly planted on the floor. When about to conduct chapel exercises he comes slowly forward, his left hand grasping his right wrist, as if the support might balance the backward tilt of his body, places his left foot nearly a yard away from the other, thrusts his head forward and with his eyes gazing at the spot where the middle foot-light would be, if there were any, begins to talk."

Shortly after Whitworth moved to Spokane, faculty established the tradition of hosting a Christmas party for all the

"While not attempting to decide for any individual what his view concerning these should be, resident students are not permitted to attend public dances or give dancing parties under the auspices of the college or any college organization."

The use of alcohol was an issue not only for Whitworth students, but for all of America as the country debated whether alcohol should be prohibited.

The Intercollegiate Prohibition Association held its annual state contest at the college and Whitworth's own Vernon Bacher came away the winner. His argument reflected the sentiments of most Whitworthians: "Again America stands in a position where she must test whether, 'a nation so conceived and so dedicated can long

Above - Gathering around the piano in McMillan Hall

Left - Mayfest dancers continued the popular tradition in Spokane

Below - All aboard: Catching the bus to Whitworth

students. Christmas carols, good food, and musical performances served as the prelude to the entrance of a faculty member dressed as Santa Claus and the exchange of gifts ranging from safety pins and sardines to sugar candy.

In the years before America's entry into the First World War, the administration still stressed in its publications the importance of Sabbath observance. But there is some evidence of modern American pluralism even as religious fundamentalism among Presbyterians and other groups began to gather momentum. In the 1916 catalogue, the college stated the following regarding social behavior: "Participation in most social amusements, such as dancing and card-playing, must be determined by the individual conscience. The college includes within its circle of friends and supporters many of widely varying views concerning the two amusements mentioned."

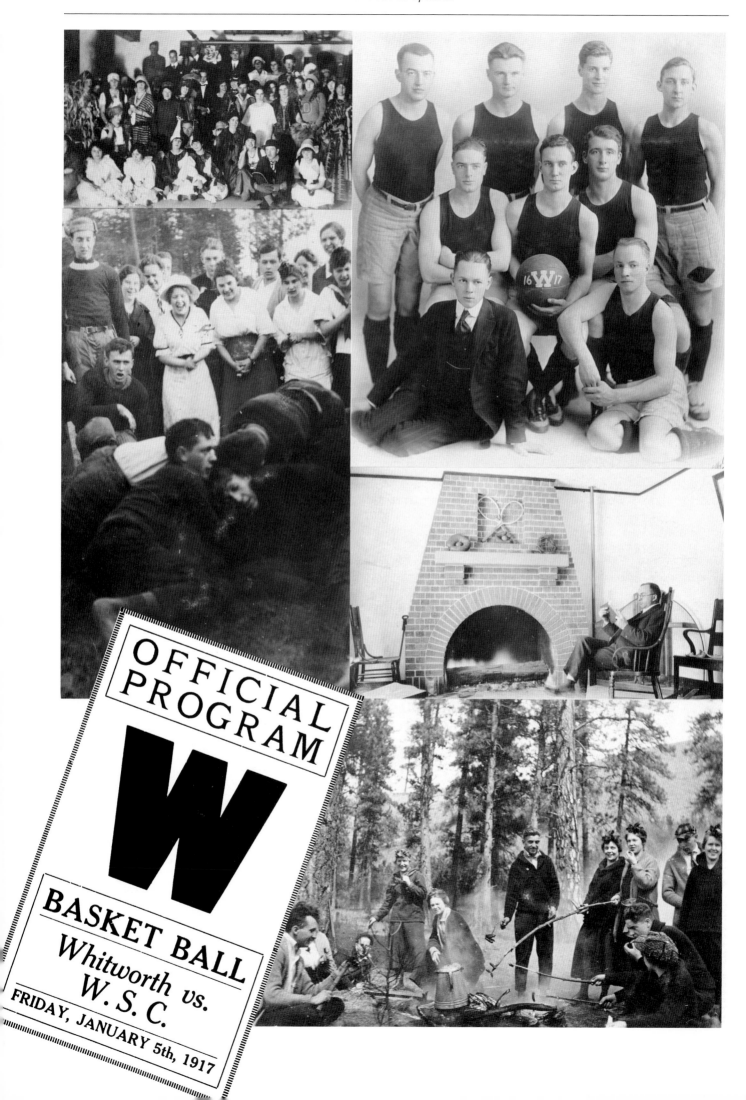

OFFICIAL PROGRAM

W

BASKET BALL
Whitworth vs.
W. S. C.
FRIDAY, JANUARY 5th, 1917

OOT BALL!!

WHITWORTH COLLEGE
vs.
DAVENPORT HIGH SCHOOL

Admission 50c   FRIDAY, OCT. 13

Feb— 1916

Above - *The Colonial Party proved to be the social event of the year.*

Right - *Colonial Party decorations*

Below, Right - *Thespians of the Drama Club*

Below, Left - *Silver Cup presented to President and Mrs. MacKay by the student body in 1917*

endure.' Although it is not always recognized as slavery, a great mass of our population has become enslaved to alcohol, for the drinker is as truly a slave as the negro was . . . . the only logical and adequate solution of the liquor problem is total abolition . . . ." — April, 1916 *Whitworthian*

On the Spokane campus, Whitworth students were much more isolated than they had been in Tacoma. Bus transportation was limited and few students owned cars. Students who lived in town could take the North Howard streetcar to one block south of Francis Avenue. From there, the Whitworth bus, with its leather seats, would pick them up and take them

to campus.

The isolation seemed to encourage a deeper sense of family. Students and faculty gathered daily in the dining hall where they discussed the politics of the day and held many theological debates. It also fostered development of school traditions and campus events.

During this period, Whitworth athletes formed the "W" club and other students formed two fraternities — Tau Beta Kappa in 1915 and Beta Pi Epsilon in 1917. Campus events and parties were the mainstays of students' social life.

The Colonial Party, with its tradition of 18th-century costumes, dominated the social calendar for many decades starting in Tacoma. In 1915, decorations included "miniature forests with the yew tree and hatchet, enticing cozy corners, and the large flag that hung above, formed by hundreds of red, white, and blue streamers. At the first chords of the orchestra the colonial dames and sires formed in line for the Grand March, which was led by Squire Guy and (speech professor) Glee Lentz. The strains of the music and its stately minuet heightened the dignity of the occasion."

In later years the Virginia Reel and Skip to M'Lou eclipsed the minuet. The mixture of folk dance (which was the only acceptable form of dance on campus) and 18th-century costuming gave this event its enduring popularity.

One of the earliest drama produc-

tions on the Spokane campus occurred in 1916 when students performed Shakespeare's *As You Like It* outside in front of the dormitories. The production honored Shakespeare on the occasion of the 300th anniversary of his death.

Reestablishing athletic traditions in Spokane was more difficult for college officials, but once they did, sporting events provided a major source of entertainment and school spirit. In 1915-16, Whitworth won two basketball games, over Spokane College, a Lutheran college on Spokane's South Hill, and Cheney Normal (now Eastern Washington University). The football team went undefeated in 1916, defeating Spokane College twice and Cheney

Above - *"As You Like It"*: This 1916 drama in the Loop celebrated the 300th anniversary of Shakespeare's death

Below - The basketball team lines up

Normal twice.

Enthusiasm for the possibilities at the Spokane site continued to abound in the next few years, but President MacKay recognized, as have all Whitworth presidents before and since, that the key to growth lay in fundraising. In 1916 and 1917, the Carnegie Foundation, the Rockefeller Education Board and the Presbyterian Board of Aid pledged a total of $125,000 if the college could raise an equal amount. President MacKay decided to go east to raise the money. But world events intervened.

In April 1917, when the United States declared war on Germany, the government asked Americans to readjust their psychological and political positions almost overnight. From the beginning of the war in 1914, Americans had been asked to remain neutral. Now President Woodrow Wilson implored his countrymen to dedicate themselves fully to the downfall of the Kaiser. The country, he told them, is engaged in a holy cause, a war to end all wars. It was a time to marshall resources and make sacrifices. At such a time, wealthy eastern philanthropists were not likely to turn their heads west and think about a small college in an obscure city.

Somehow, the Whitworth trustees failed to grasp the effect of the war on their agenda; instead, they insisted that Dr. MacKay press forward with the campaign. MacKay disagreed and tendered his resignation. Because the school newspaper did not publish during 1917-1918, it is difficult to read the mood of the campus, but there must have been considerable consternation on the part of the faculty, because nine members resigned along

with Dr. MacKay.

These events took a toll on long-range plans for the college. When the hopes for a successful campaign failed to materialize, the result was that two dormitories and a temporary gymnasium were to be the only major buildings on campus until the 1940s.

Even so, the 1917-1918 school year opened on an optimistic note as enrollment was higher than predicted. Operational finances seemed reasonably sound. But by the time the new president, the Reverend B. Scott Bates, took office on February 1, 1918, the enrollment had declined as young men from the college enlisted in the army.

One can only speculate whether Whitworth students were any more or less prepared for their war experiences than their peers. Some of them surely shared feelings like those of Erich Maria Remarque. In *All Quiet on the Western Front*, Remarque wrote for an entire generation about disillusionment with the educational values of western civilization. It grew difficult to argue that Greek and Latin ought to be at the core of the curriculum. The demands of combat and the rigors of military life dictated that college life and the educational process would

have to change after the war.

The effect of the war became more stark with the report of Whitworth's first war casualty, Harry Olson, who died in action on September 21, 1918.

By August 1918, Whitworth had incurred a $13,500 deficit and the trustees decided to close the school and lease the campus and buildings to the U. S. Government for an auto-tractor school. The college released the president and faculty to find work elsewhere. The future was indeed uncertain; temporarily, at least, the events in northern France placed a hold on George Whitworth's dream.

Above - A busy parking lot in front of Ballard Hall

Below - Home Economics : Women learn to prepare meals

Chapter IV - The 1920s

Struggling To Rebuild

*W*hile many Americans in the post-war years danced to the tunes of the Jazz Age, listened to this curiosity called "the wireless," and attended sporting events in record numbers, Whitworth faculty and administrators worried about the college's future. The cultural ferment following World War I forced colleges to reexamine curricula and their assumptions about how students should incorporate the new with the old. But for Whitworth, there was a greater problem—simply surviving. Not since the first years of its existence had the dream of George Whitworth been in such jeopardy.

The U. S. Army Tractor School had made a shambles of the dormitories. Whitworth College existed in name only; there were no faculty, no president, and

no students. More than a few responsible people argued that the only reasonable course was to merge Whitworth with two other struggling Protestant colleges in the city, Spokane College and Spokane University.

The person most opposed to merger was Trustee Mark Allison Matthews, pastor of Seattle's First Presbyterian Church. Always a strong leader, he had been accused of meddling in the college's hiring and firing during the Tacoma years. Now a former moderator of the General Assembly, and leader of the denomination's largest church, he was one of the half-dozen most famous and powerful Presbyterians in the country.

At Matthews' insistence, merger plans were quashed, and along with Dr.

Facing Page - Blackened Ballard: Students watched their home burn and sang the alma mater

Below - Class of '24: Enrollment dropped as Whitworth struggled to survive

Arthur Beatie, he helped raise $75,000 pledged over a three-year period. The trustees reconstituted themselves and made the decision to restart classes on September 16, 1919. Beatie's success at raising funds led the board to offer him the presidency. He accepted.

Almost immediately, President Beatie headed east to recruit faculty. Returning World War I veterans increased the demand for college courses, and in the first post-war year there were 98 college-level students. Of these, 40 were day school students and 58 were in the evening extension classes held at the city library.

Dr. Beatie's tenure was short. He resigned after only ten months amidst charges that the Board of Trustees was sidestepping its responsibilities and counter-charges that he was suspending and expelling students without faculty approval and, moreover, his sermons were too long. Yet enrollment was the best since moving to Spokane.

Professor Charles Barry served as acting president until March 1921, when he died of a sudden illness. He was succeeded by Professor Willard Robinson, head of the Greek and Bible department. His sister, Miss Edna Moor Robinson, was head of the Whitworth English Department and associate dean of women.

Robinson's first task as president

Facing Page ,Top -
Carried away: Presi-
dent Willard Robinson
lifted by students in
front of McMillan Hall

Facing Page, Center -
Ballard Hall after 1927
fire

Facing Page, Bottom
President Walter
Stevenson and Dean
Orrin Tiffany amid the
ruins of Ballard Hall

Left - Whitworth's
library in McMillan
Hall

Below - Dean Orrin
Tiffany

was to secure enough money to pay the faculty back salary and keep the college afloat. After he had experienced some initial success, the General Education Board of the General Assembly came to Spokane to launch a $1,000,000 campaign for Whitworth. Once again the drive stalled, in part because of strained relations between Dr. Robinson, the faculty, and the board's executive committee. One former student recalled the atmosphere as chaotic; students flouted the administration by leading a cow to the third floor of McMillan Hall. On April 3, 1923, Robinson and his sister resigned.

Many observers doubted the college would reopen in the fall of 1923. No contracts were issued to faculty members. Board members resigned and the Synod assigned a special five-member commission to make recommendations. Again, Mark Matthews spearheaded the group, urging the Presbyterian Synod to renew commitment to support the college with students and money.

The board named Dr. Walter A. Stevenson, pastor of Mizpah Presbyterian Church, Portland, Oregon, to be the next president. Over the next two years, he helped restore the financial stability of the college.

Then, at 2:45 a.m. on March 8, 1927, Carl Boppell, a senior living on the

Above - *Whitworth's bus took students from campus to town*

Below Right - *Bus stop at McMillan Hall*

Below Left - *President Walter Stevenson (1923-1927)*

third floor of Ballard Hall, discovered a fire. With his roommate, Donald Beal, Boppell awakened the 18 other male students. They immediately began to remove their belongings and what furniture they could. Alumna Kathryn Bockman recalled how startled she was when she awakened in McMillan Hall and found her "windows were red with a strange light. . . . Boys were running and calling to each other. Some were carrying bedding and all sorts of property to all parts of the already strewn campus."

When fire engines arrived, firefighters concentrated on saving McMillan as a fierce wind sprayed sparks toward the other building. In the bitter cold, students gathered on the lawn outside and watched the blaze consume Ballard Hall and, with it, Dean Orrin Tiffany's extensive library.

One student recalled singing while the fire raged. "When we sent our 'Alma Mater' ringing out, a hard, huge lump filled our throats and a mist spread before our eyes."

Alumna Gladys Tattersall later wrote, "I remembered the many little social affairs given in the men's living room, the glowing fire and marshmallow roasts, the games played and programs enjoyed, and as I gazed, I felt a poignant clutching at my heart as if I had lost an old friend."

Later that morning in chapel, Dean Orrin Tiffany spoke of the spirit of courage he'd observed hours before. Then he read a telegram from President Stevenson, who was away from campus. In it, the president pledged to build a new and

Left - *Rev. Mark Mat-thews: Seattle pastor, social reformer and Whitworth trustee*

Below - *Faculty members: Economics and sociology professor Herbert Hussong (l) and mathematics professor Walter Buxton (r)*

Bottom - *The 1928 Faculty Club*

greater Whitworth. With that, pent-up feeling among the students burst forth into tremendous applause.

Five days after the fire, the entire student body arose at 6 a.m. to meet President Stevenson's train as he returned to Spokane and to take him home for breakfast.

Classes moved into McMillan Hall or the president's home, and women students "doubled up" in rooms on the second floor of McMillan so the men could take over the third floor. Men made their entrances and exits to their new home by way of the fire escapes.

Merchants and the Spokane community in general responded generously to the plight of the school and students, providing clothing and supplies. Churches opened their doors to several students.

After the fire, discussion resumed about merger with the Lutheran college on the South Hill, as it was also having financial difficulties. The Board of Christian Education of the General Assembly urged merger if Whitworth could not muster more support.

Apparently taking this as a vote of no confidence, President Stevenson announced his resignation, to the surprise and disappointment of most of the student body. Stevenson's tenure had brought significant progress; the school had been reaccredited and the financial situation had improved. Stevenson was particularly pleased with his influence on the religious life at the college.

The merger issue faced opposition from several strong voices on the board: the Reverends Charles Boppell and Mark Matthews, and Dr. Frank Chalmers McKean, pastor of Spokane's First Presbyterian Church. Matthews once again was particularly persuasive with representatives of the General Board of Christian Education.

After many months of waffling, the Synod committed its support in July 1927. New con-

Above - "Then as now, on warm fall and spring days, classes have been held in the Loop"

Below - "Procerpina": Cast from student drama production

struction on Ballard Hall began in August and school opened only one week late. The board appointed Dean Orrin Tiffany, professor of history, as acting president. Only six of the thirteen faculty had taught during the previous year, and only 57 students enrolled in 1927-1928.

Whitworth's difficulties in the 1920s caused instability among both administration and faculty. Six presidents, permanent or acting, held office during the decade. Nevertheless, there were faculty members who significantly affected the lives of Whitworth students during that time.

Professor Herbert Hussong was one of the great favorites. A professional baseball player in his earlier years, he sparked class discussion in economics and sociology with anecdotes from the world of sports. As second violinist in the

school orchestra and occasionally its director, he held the orchestra together by the force of his personality. Sixty years later, Burton Belknap recalled the night he invited Professor Hussong up to his house for dinner and conversation with the not-so-subtle hope that his grade would improve — and indeed, it seemed to work.

Professor Walter Buxton, a gifted scholar in mathematics, was known for being conversant on wide-ranging subjects. History Professor Orton Carmichael had been on the faculty less that a year when the 1925 *Natsihi* staff dedicated the yearbook to him, praising his quiet, unassuming character and his ability to point students "to the God of Nature by unfolding the Power of Love of God in Nature." Three years later, after his untimely death, the class of 1928 donated funds to erect the Carmichael Memorial Pillars at the cam-

The Senior Sneak

With Laudenbach at the gear shift,
  We're outward bound today.
It matters not what glistening lake,
  Hayden or Coeur d'Alene.

We're sick of stuffy school rooms,
  Of work, and books, and grind.
Give us the blue of the open lake
  For the classroom every time.

You can have your dull old French book
  For it's all Greek to me.
Give me a little rowboat
  Where I can feel I'm free.

A swayin' through the water
  Like a rollin', drunken dray,
A hammered, battered little tub,
  Will bring us back today.

And when she does there's waiting
  A memory to store
'Mong those happy days soon over
  That will come to us no more.

And if she won't, she won't then,
  And I'd just as soon be there
As in some shady school house
  With professor in his lair.

So rent the little rowboat
  We're outward bound today.
And let us all remember, we're on
  The Senior Sneak. Hooray!

—ARTHUR ROBERTS.

pus entrance.

Whitworth students and faculty, like most Americans, struggled with the onset of "modernism" in many forms during the decade. Campus debate swirled over subjects like the teaching of evolution. After the celebrated "Scopes Monkey Trial" in the summer of 1925, administrators felt compelled in the 1926 catalogue to note that the college "teaches that the Creator's works in nature are never at variance with his revelation in the Bible when both are fully understood."

At other times during the decade, students and faculty debated the merits of jazz music. On one occasion, at least one student's dismay was reflected in the 1923 *Natsihi*.

"The pestilence of modern times in the music line has noteworthily left its stamp on Whitworth this year. From the beginning of the school term to its finish has this craze imbedded itself in the students, for it is jazz before and after break-

Below - First gymnasium at north end of Pine Bowl. Known as the "Arctic zone," the Gym wasn't heated in early years

Left - Senior Sneak poem from 1928 Natsihi

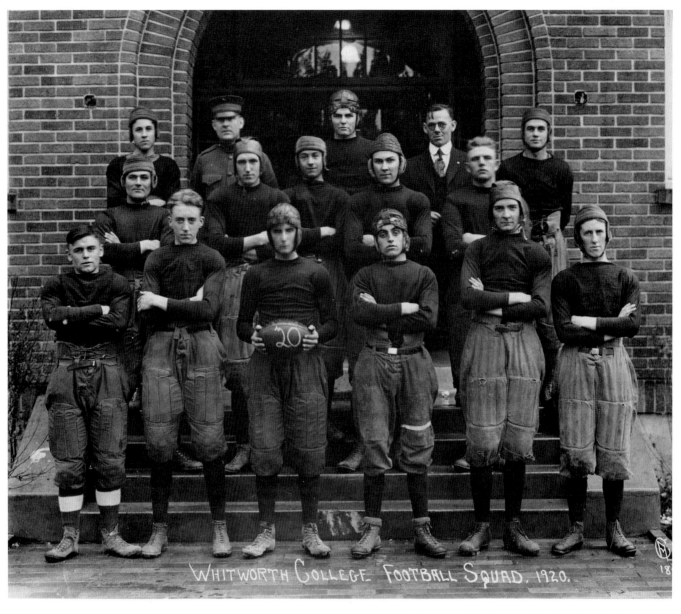

WHITWORTH COLLEGE FOOTBALL SQUAD. 1920.

fast, jazz before and after lunch, between times and for dinner."

During the decade other students voiced their concern over the future of America and its profligate life style:

"As a nation of people we are living in an age of luxury, modernism, and aberration, which will eventually be our perdition. Statistics present to us the fact that, of the entire money in circulation in America, only one and one fourth per cent is spent on the church . . . . Among the younger generation we see an asinine thinking taking the place of serious thought, and numerous frivolities being substituted for salutary amusements." — May 18, 1927 *Whitworthian*.

Whitworth students did not all share a desire to retain the traditional ways when it came to separating the sexes. One *Whitworthian* editorial in January 1922 suggested that the college should have a "Spooning Parlor."

"It is...very embarrassing to entertain one another with the public a witness to every move that is made or every word that is said . . . . Therefore, we suggest a solution to the great problem before us. The first thing we think of is . . . a 'spooning parlor.' This parlor would contain the various comforts of home. It would also have the 'cozy corners' in which a young woman or young man may entertain his or her admirer. In this way the lovers could open their soul to their hearts' content and not be interrupted, or feel embarrassed by having an audience. By no means would scandal be permitted, for in charge of the parlor would be a real Christian matron who understands the passions of young men and young women."

Student newspapers and annuals of the time reflect a balance between seriousness about the world and a desire simply to enjoy one another's company. As far as we know, no spooning parlor was ever created.

Still lacking a formal mascot for the college, the Whitworth student body grew tired of having its teams referred to as the "Presbyterians" or the "Preachers," and in the spring of 1926 suggested the following names: Lynx, Spartans, Tigers, Bantams, Bobcats, Panthers, Huns, and Trojans. A group of athletes suggested the name Pirates, which carried the day.

Student organizations thrived. The Criterion Literary Society, the YMCA and YWCA, the Kappa Gammas, Tri-G's, Women's Athletic Association, Volunteer Fellowship, Alpha Psi Delta, and Sigma Theta became outlets for service activity and religious fellowship. The French Club, under the direction of Professor Beatrice Barnes, was also a favorite.

A great yearly event emerged with the availability of the automobile — the Senior Sneak. Each spring, the entire senior class left campus for a secret location on Hayden or Coeur d'Alene Lake. Often, the junior class would give chase through the countryside hoping to find the rendezvous, usually without success.

The students' Volunteer Fellowship made frequent weekend trips to neighboring communities. Students led hymn singing, prayers, Scripture reading, and sang in duets or quartets. A large community dinner and an afternoon service would follow.

The Whitworth Gospel Team, an outgrowth of the YMCA program, developed into one of the most dynamic programs on campus. During its first year, the Gospel Team appeared before nearly 4,000 young people throughout eastern Washington and effectively conveyed the

Facing Page, Top -
1920 football team:
Few victories, but spirited play

Facing Page, Bottom
1921 basketball team:
Women's sports thrived
during the 1920s

Above - Champs of
1922: Baseball squad
won the Spokane Inter-
collegiate Conference
Championship

Above - Women's recreation class on the baseball diamond

spirit of Whitworth College.

The campus YWCA chapter hosted an annual winter carnival that in effect was a huge vaudeville show, with Japanese dance, solo dances, musical duets, and skits. Sideshow acts included Bluebeard, a Rogues gallery, Seven Wonders of the World, a hairless dog, and the greatest monkey in the world.

Campus Day began in the Tacoma years, but became a major event in the teens and '20s. Each fall and spring, students, faculty, and local trustees would gather on a Saturday to put the campus in shape. Students and faculty gathered for a beefsteak breakfast at Lake Wandermere before the work. "Smoke, bonfires, rakes, wheelbarrows, horses, trustees, and students in working garb were to be found on the campus," said an April 1916 *Whitworthian.* Students cleared underbrush and planted trees, shrubs, and flowers. They swept gym floors, smoothed athletic fields, and groomed the grounds with hoes and rakes borrowed from nearby neighbors. "Even the Dean forgot to wear a coat and appeared in shirt sleeves," the paper reported. When all was finished, students, faculty and trustees gathered for a big lunch on the lawn, followed by a football game in the afternoon.

The Glee Club, which included students and faculty, provided outstanding musical programs. Professor Frank

Tattersall and Miss Dorothy Farr (Mrs.Grant Dixon, Sr.) directed the group in operettas such as *Patricia, Sylvia,* and *Sailor Maids.* Drama productions included *She Stoops to Conquer, The Top Landing, Come Out of the Kitchen,* and *Daddy Long Legs.* Debate was also popular; in 1928 Whitworth won the league conference.

The football team won five of six games in 1921, losing only to Cheney Normal College. In 1922, Whitworth won the Spokane Intercollegiate Conference championship. But a dip in enrollment during the decade took its toll. During the next five seasons Whitworth won only six of 20 games.

Basketball started again in 1920, but was cancelled after only two games because of a flu epidemic. In January 1922, builders finished a new gymnasium, but it was unheated. Students referred to it as the "Arctic Zone." When fans packed into the balcony, however, it turned into the torrid zone. *The Whitworthian,* reporting on a game against Spokane College, said that student spirit "made rafters rock with their vociferous rooting. The Whitworth spirit to win was in every loyal son's heart that memorable night, and that was one of the reasons why our boys made the opposing team look like store window dummies." Whitworth won 23 to 21.

While competition was fierce, the post-game atmosphere differed from

today's. After a Lewiston basketball game in 1927, for example, the Whitworth women provided a meal for both teams and in return the players serenaded them.

In 1922, the Whitworth baseball team won the Spokane Intercollegiate Conference championship under Coach Abe Cohn. The track and tennis teams also had winning seasons.

Women played intercollegiate tennis and basketball, and intramural baseball, basketball, and tennis. In 1922, Dorothy Farr, Delilah Barber, and Sarah Miller received letters for intercollegiate competition. Miss Farr was conference tennis champion in 1922 and 1923; Lindalee Miller reached the intercollegiate singles finals in 1926.

Enrollments were unstable in the 1920s and the graduating class of 1926 consisted of only two women, Dorothy Brenton and Thelma Porter. But their lists of activities reveal the breadth and commitment of student leaders of the day and the opportunities afforded by a small enrollment. Dorothy was a member of Kappa Gamma, Volunteer Fellowship, the Gospel Team, Pyramid Literary Society, Women's Athletic Association Executive Board, and the volleyball team in 1926. She was in the following school productions: *The Littlest Bridesmaid*, *Why Not Jim*, *Sylvia*, and *Daddy Long Legs*.

Thelma Porter was president of

Kappa Gamma, a *Natsihi* staff writer, a member in the Literary Society, an Executive Board member of the Student Association, president of the Women's Athletic Association, and class president. She started the YWCA campus chapter in 1922. A Glee Club singer, Thelma performed in the dramatic productions of *Littlest Bridesmaid* and *Daddy Long Legs*.

Low enrollment eventually reduced students' opportunities. Kappa Gamma, the oldest college organization, and two fraternities—Alpha Psi Delta and Kappa Omicron Sigma—were forced to disband in 1928 when the Board of Trustees, at the urging of President Tiffany, banned sororities and fraternities until the enrollment should reach 200.

Though much of what had happened during the decade was encouraging, the future of the college was uncertain at its close. The Great Depression would soon appear and another period of struggle would face students, faculty, and administration.

Above - *Tennis team of 1923*

Left - *The "W" Club athletic organization*

CHAPTER V - THE 1930s

THE GREAT DEPRESSION

Troubled times were nothing new to Whitworth College. While it managed to stay intact despite merger threats and near failures in the 1920s, brighter days still seemed distant when the Reverend Dr. Ward Sullivan became the college's eleventh president in 1929. Sullivan had been the dean of Albany College in Oregon. In one of his first actions as Whitworth's president, he hired Ford Bailor, a former Spokane University coach, as an executive assistant. Bailor would be responsible for enhancing admissions and promoting the college. His energy and enthusiasm proved invaluable in building the student body.

Sullivan also named Francis Hardwick dean. It was perhaps his most important appointment. Born in England, Hardwick earned a doctorate from the University of Washington at the age of 60. A linguist, mathematician, and psychologist, Dean Hardwick felt at home in scientific fields and was well-versed in literature. The Presbyterian Church ordained him at age 68. He learned Russian and became an experimental psychologist in his 70s.

Even though he occasionally took them to task, the students were very fond of Dean Hardwick. Years later, one student remembered the kindly manner in which Dr. Hardwick explained the evils of smoking "double-humped dromedaries" (a reference to Camel cigarettes). Students honored Hardwick in 1957 by naming the student union building after him.

The '30s were marked by a greater sense of stability than previous decades. The college was fully accredited and class enrollment began to rise, largely due to the efforts of Bailor. In 1929-30, only 81 students attended, but by 1939 the count had reached 264. In addition to Bailor's efforts, trustees William McEachran and Albert Arend played a strong role in the life of the college during those years. And,

Facing Page - Anticipation: Paddling was a common initiation of the 1930s.

Below Left - William L. McEachran: Chairman of the Board of Trustees (1923-1959)

Below Right - President Ward Sullivan (1929-1938) in front of (l to r) Dean Francis Hardwick, Dan Fleming and Dr. Hedrick

Above - Trustee
Albert Arend

Above Right - *Winter at Whitworth in 1933*

Below - *Say Cheese: The faculty and student body pose for a campus portrait*

perhaps because of the Depression, faculty members chose to stay longer in their positions than faculty had in Whitworth's earlier decades.

While most Whitworth students did not dwell on the Depression, nevertheless, it remained in the background. Student editors occasionally commented on its impact on their lives. "The undergraduate is facing his studies with the realization that 'life is real and earnest' — and they all blame it on the good old depression! Perhaps all these college au-

thorities are right. We who are in college are doing a little rejoicing ourselves. We've decided that this is a good time to be in college. If we were out in the cold, cruel, and depressed Wide World, we probably couldn't get a job, and so we think that it sounds like a good idea to spend this 'depression period' preparing ourselves for a job when we get out of college and the depression is over. We're just one of those lucky persons." —*Whitworthian* November 18, 1932

During the Depression, students

Left - Graduation Day 1930

Below Left - 1930s students were required to say "Hello" when passing on this walkway between Ballard and McMillan

Below Right - May Day court: A campus tradition

Above - *Easy riders: Motorcycles were a popular way to get around*

Below - Ocarina Trio provided Depression era entertainment

found a marvelous array of part-time jobs to make money. Grant Rodkey was the college barber during his years at school, and Carl Blanford worked his way through as the college printer. On his press in an old shed behind Ballard Hall, Blanford printed publications ranging from *The Whitworthian* to college promotional materials. Beatrice Henderson reports that she picked and canned 742 quarts of fruit during one summer to pay for her first year's tuition. Others paid tuition in applesauce, potatoes and, from one student, peanut butter. Dining hall patrons that year ate peanut butter bread, peanut butter cookies, peanut butter pancakes and peanut butter soup.

Entertaining themselves took some creativity in those days when students had little money. The Spokane environs offered lots of places for a hike or picnic, and a group could

always carpool to a movie. But often students' lack of resources confined them to campus, and then they relied on clubs to provide social activities. In the dorms, radio filled evening hours with detective mysteries such as the "The Shadow," and the comedies of Fred Allen, Jack Benny, and Burns and Allen.

An April 1933 issue of *The Whitworthian* revealed one solution to the problem of not enough money, and combined it with a tongue-in-cheek answer to America's economic woes. "The committee on arrangements was in desperate

straits, when, lo and behold, some brain began to function. A wiener roast didn't have to require gas, money, or memories after all — the party could walk!! And that is where saving the American shoe industry comes in. Even the best of walking parties is bound to wear out shoe leather."

The 1935 Student Handbook reflected the efforts on the part of the administration to cut costs wherever possible. "Students using extra light and electrical appliances will be subject to regulation and charges. One person in a room will be allowed two electric lights; two persons, three electric lights. For additional lights or electrical appliances an extra charge will be made. The use of electric irons or hot plates is not permitted in dormitory rooms."

Salaries were pitiful and faculty occasionally went unpaid. Chairman of the Board of Trustees William McEachran, who owned a chain of 40 food stores, often donated groceries for the dining hall and put bags of groceries together for families of faculty until they could be paid. Nevertheless, faculty from the period, such as Leslie Hedrick, recall their

camaraderie and *esprit de corps.* "None of us had any money during those days, we never knew when we were going to get any more, hence we could not run a charge account, so we scrimped and saved the best we could, but we had some wonderful times with other faculty members and with the students and still some of our best friends are the ones we met at Whit-

Above - Chapel attendance was compulsory and faculty sat up on the stage

Below - German band provided "Oompah" music for events

worth." (Gray p. 142)

Humor helped. The Hardwicks hosted a faculty hobo party. The dean, in tattered costume and unshaven face, was voted the King of the Hobo Camp.

Organizations flourished during the '30s: Volunteer Fellowship, the W-Club, Women's Athletic Association, the Philadelphians, Christian Endeavor, Sefelo (which was derived from SErvice, FEllowship, and LOve), and Pirettes. Dean Marion Jenkins had arrived at Whitworth in 1931 and shortly thereafter began to advise the Pirettes, a women's pep and service organization. Dean Jenkins would come to influence hundreds of students during her thirty-four year

career at the college.

In the spring of 1933, students celebrated St. Patrick's Day with an event called the Green Derby. A ten-piece jazz band played during the chapel period; cutting the Green Derby cake at noon was the climax.

The event featured vaudeville acts — magic, ventriloquism, tumbling, and gymnastics. Kelly's Hat Band and a German band played. Decorations included a large green bowler of crepe paper suspended above the stage at the rear of the auditorium. In 1934, Albert Arend was master of ceremonies. The entertainment included piano solos, a Roman ladder act, tap dancers, marionettes, a women's trio,

British Isles bagpipes, accordion music, and blues singers.

Membership in the "W" Club offered men high visibility on campus. Initiation requirements included "no talking to women for a week, and each inductee had to perform in chapel. John Normark had to read a love poem and Clarence Smith Coolbs sang the popular song, 'I Fa' Down an' Go Boom.' Bill Daut gave a speech, 'How I Became the Athlete that I Am,'and Jack Mott pontificated on 'The Girl of My Dreams.' Hedley Vicker gave his rendition of a love poem and Bert Schwartz orated on the subject of prohibition. Walt Petsch and Harvey Long performed Swiss yodeling. Paddles were used during the week to remind initiates that they had not performed their obligations adequately." — *Whitworthian*, January 7, 1932.

The long tradition of a men's quartet started in the 1930s. The first one consisted of Loren Hatcher, Mark Koehler (future president of the college), Keith Murray, and Paul Koper. Each received $75 a semester and a dress suit from the college. The four young men travelled the region, developing an excellent reputation and serving as outstanding ambassadors for the institution.

Another tradition was formalized in 1931 when ASWC passed regulations for freshman initiates: ". . . the first quarter, they shall wear the green cap, shall not enter the front door, shall go last to the dining room, shall address the upperclassmen as Mr., Mrs., or Miss, . . . and shall be under the jurisdiction of the Sophomore men. Freshman girls shall wear the green ribbon with the hair behind the ears, use no cosmetics, wear no high-heeled shoes, enter the front door, address upperclassmen and Sophomores as Mr., Miss, or Mrs., and are not to speak to a gentleman during school hours unless business demands . . . ."

In 1932, students chose "Hail Whitworth Hail," written by Lawrence Mitchell, to be the new alma mater. Students first heard Dorothy Farr sing it at a Whitworth banquet.

Hail! Whitworth College,
Hail ever hail,
Long may thy banner victorious wave;
Thy sons and daughters, loyal and brave,
Hail thee forever, Hail, Whitworth, Hail!

Above - *The big freshman-sophomore battle started off the school year*

Left - *Pyrotechnics: Homecoming bonfires were spectacular*

Hail, Alma Mater, mighty and true,
Onward together, strive for the right.
Courage unfailing, strength for the fight,
Hail thee forever, Hail, Whitworth, Hail!

Harold Eastburg, a freshman, wrote the fight song, which the student body adopted in 1932.

For Whitworth Fight!
Fight! Fight and win!
For the Crimson and Black,
The highest honors bring back.
For Whitworth Fight!
Fight! Hear the cry,
"Onward to Victory."
Be not content with less,
Whitworth deserves the best.
So Pirates. Fight! Fight! Fight! and Win!

Homecoming in the 1930s was an elaborate affair. It typically began on Friday morning with an alumni convocation with stunts, stories, and pep talks. That

Above - *Long-time professor Benjamin Neustel surrounded by glass bottles in the chemistry lab*

Right - *Low rent district: Lee and Grant Rodkey move into makeshift living quarters*

evening, students would lead a pep rally with a serpentine, pep talks by cheer leaders, faculty members and alumni, and lots of cheers and college songs. Then came the major spectacle: the Frosh bonfire. After Saturday's big game, usually against rival Spokane University, a banquet climaxed the weekend.

Even in the 1930s, however, students felt that some of their colleagues lacked school spirit. "At a recent basketball game," wrote one, "there were more rooters for the opposing team than for Whitworth.... The other day in assembly, when the yell leader asked for a little pep, there were plenty of "boos" from the associated students. How's that for college spirit? . . . ." --*Whitworthian*, February 22, 1934.

In 1938, controversy arose between President Sullivan and Dean Hardwick

on a number of issues. Under pressure from the faculty, Sullivan resigned in June 1938, but the board refused to accept his resignation and told the two to work out their differences. Sullivan resigned again in September 1938. This time the board accepted his resignation, as the faculty clearly sided with the dean. Dr. Hardwick served as acting president in 1939.

But the '30s had been a period of relative stability among the faculty under the leadership of President Sullivan. His tenure as president from 1929 to 1938 was the longest in the college's history. The days of high faculty turnover seemed to be at an end. Of those hired during Sullivan's administration, ten faculty members were with the college more than ten years: Hardwick, Benjamin Neustel, James W. Countermine, Helen Magill, Dean Marion Jenkins, Estella Baldwin, Winifred

Above - *Pirettes: One of the most popular women's service organizations in Whitworth history*

Left - *Whitworth choir of 1936: Tradition of regional tours began under Winifred McNair Hopkins' direction*

Hopkins, Gerald Stannard, Anna J. Carrel, and John A. Carlson. Of these, five were to be with the college for more than a quarter century: Baldwin (37 years), Carlson (36), Jenkins (34), Neustel (28), and Carrel (27).

Graduates of the era speak with enormous respect and fondness for members of the faculty. Grant Rodkey, '39, who went on to Harvard Medical School, recalled how moved he felt when faculty members, knowing he lacked the necessary money, paid his $50 entrance fee to Harvard. In addition, Dr. Countermine sent Rodkey off to Harvard with the professor's only typewriter.

The curriculum expanded during the 1930s. While only five departments offered more than 10 courses in 1928, 14 departments were in this category by 1939. While the faculty of 1930 described the college as a liberal arts institution "giving a broad cultural background for a virile Christian citizenship," it also arranged the curriculum to train students for definite vocations and to give pre-professional instruction to those desiring it. In addition to the liberal arts majors, the college offered majors in business administration, pre-dentistry, pre-engineering, pre-medicine, and pre-pharmacy. To these they added nurses' training in 1931 and pre-law in 1933.

During this period, the music

Top *- The faculty of 1933: A source of stability in tough times*

Above *- The 1936 Orchestra, directed by George Poinar (lower left)*

department began to grow under the direction of Grace Soltau and Hungarian-born George Poinar, a top-rated violinist and conductor. Poinar had become a popular Spokane concert artist and had established the local civic symphony orchestra. After Poinar's resignation in 1938, Arthur E. Uhe, who had been a Victor recording artist and first violinist of the Chicago-Philadelphia Opera Association and the Royal Opera of Brussels, took his place on the Whitworth staff.

Other music faculty members who came during the 1930s were Anna J. Carrel, organ and piano instructor, and Winifred McNair Hopkins, who began the Whitworth tradition of choir tours with productions of *The Messiah* and *The Crucifixion*. As a result of the excellent music program, several students went on to outstanding musical careers and the college's reputation grew.

Whitworth athletics also made great strides during the decade. In 1934, Jerry Stannard took over the football coaching duties and would stay in the position for five years, the longest stint in the history of the college to that point. Stannard later told how he met seven players that first season equipped only with pre-World War I football gear. Stannard liked to remind people about his 123-pound guard and the fact that before the first game he still could be sure of only seven players. Thirteen years later, a *Whitworthian* reporter, recounting the story, described Stannard's solution:

"When the whistle sounded for the opening kick-off, Coach Stannard had eleven red shirts facing the opposition. It is not known to this day whom he drafted, but they say that four men on the faculty came to school with the aid of canes and crutches the following morning." *Whitworthian,* October 3, 1947.

The first Whitworth athletic trophy, funded in 1931 by professors David and Grace Soltau, was the James Snider Memorial Award. The preceding football season had been cut short by Snider's sudden death from pneumonia. The first award went to Arthur Roberts and Ray Lavender.

Whitworth football reached a high point in 1938 with the selection of guard Norman Richardson to the Williamson Little All-American first team.

This was Whitworth's first national sports award, and its importance was underscored by the fact that Richardson was the only first team selection from west of the Mississippi. Too shy to accept the award, the young star persuaded his identical twin brother, Leonard (also a star on the team), to attend the ceremonies. No one but the brothers and Coach Stannard knew the difference.

Whitworth basketball teams had a greater percentage of victories than the football squads, but they played most games against locally sponsored, independent teams. Clifford Bromling, Dutch Krueger, Harvey Long, Tommy Ventris,

Mark Koehler, Harold Penhalurick, and Elmer Douglas played major roles during the 1930s. When the Pirates established their inspirational award for basketball in 1935, Mark Koehler received the honor.

The *Natsihi* mentioned women's basketball often from 1929 through 1934, but success measured in wins proved elusive. The activity of the Women's Athletic Association through the decade,

Top - Frosty football: Coach Jerry Stannard's offense takes off

Above *- Basketball team of 1933*

under the leadership of Mrs. Hedrick, director of women's physical education, engaged most of the Whitworth women. In addition to a lot of hiking, women played archery, tennis, volleyball, badminton, shuffleboard, and darts.

In 1934-35, Whitworth debate teams won seven out of nine debate decisions. At a tournament held at Whitworth in 1935, the Pirates tied Gonzaga and Washington State College for first place.

The high point for oratory was Lorraine Rasco's first place award in 1937 in a national contest sponsored by the Presbyterian Board of Foreign Missions. For topping 2,000 other contestants, Miss Rasco received a 10-week trip to Asia. She also won first honors in oratory at Linfield, Oregon, while Mary Virginia Mount took first place in extemporaneous and after-dinner speaking. In 1939, Miss Mount won first in senior women's oratory at a tournament sponsored by the Western Association of Teachers of Speech.

The onset of war in Europe in September 1939 brought few immediate changes to the Whitworth campus. Religious Emphasis Week proceeded in the usual manner in the spring of 1940. But evidence of a growing consciousness of the European conflict began to seep into various Whitworth activities, even if at first it was only tongue-in-cheek–like this description of the 1940 senior sneak: "Striking with the rapidity of a German blitzkrieg, but moving noisily as a company of Russian tanks, the senior forces of Whitworth College evacuated the campus and invaded the territory around Diamond Lake, attempting to purge the juniors from their midst. Hostilities and festivities broke out about dawn on April 24, that fateful day. It was a cold morning the seniors stole away, but the juniors were hot on their trail. Much credit for apprehending the seniors goes to Edith Purcell, who is now writing a book entitled 'Confessions of a Junior Spy.' Two of the junior special agents, Fred Burnett and Pinky Unti, deserve to be awarded the debate team's cup for discovering Ed Bassford and Gene

Muench, trying to hide behind the same small pine tree. Well, pal, the juniors located the seniors and 'der Fuehrer,' Stan Hughart, around noon; and an alliance was suggested by Pinky Unti and Harriet Badon.

"This peace pact was signed by Gladys Hawley and Werner Rosenquist; and by Edith Purcell and Gene Muench. Then the rains came. The remainder of the morning was spent playing "crack-the-whip" and in singing such old time ballads as "Who Put the Overalls in Mother Murphy's Chowder?" Food cards were abolished for the day, and everybody ate like John Law.

"The highlight of the afternoon was a rough and ragged softball game between the two classes. Although the seniors won the game, Junior Louie Stannard hit the ball so far that when it came back it was autographed by Mayor Langlie of Seattle. Many students engaged in rowing and bailing on the lake, while others fought mosquitoes on shore.

"In the evening by the fire, everybody relaxed except Lew Kirsch — who doesn't know how — and 58 young people sang as they had never sung before — that is to say, they sang well. After singing many old popular songs, the group seemed to turn naturally to peppy choruses and well-loved hymns. Everyone had a fine time, and went home agreeing that 'It was more fun than a picnic.'" *Whitworthian*, May 8, 1940

Whitworth students expressed their political opinions in a straw vote in October 1940, one month before the presidential election. Students voted overwhelmingly for Wendell Wilkie over Franklin Roosevelt, 159 to 103. The faculty was 6 to 4 for Wilkie. Interestingly, eight students (five per cent) voted for Earl Browder, running on the communist ticket, and three per cent voted for Norman Thomas, a socialist.

Wilkie visited Spokane in September 1940, and was interviewed by a Whitworth student, who asked if college students would be exempt from the draft. Wilkie replied, "Certainly!"

Whitworth students mainly had their minds on campus and their studies, but before long, events in Europe and in the Pacific would shift their attention elsewhere.

In 1939, Whitworth College looked

Above - *Upperclass shoeshine: Another initiation ritual for freshmen*

Left - *Basketball team of 1935*

forward to celebrating a half-century of existence. From its origins in Sumner to its move to Tacoma and subsequently Spokane, administrators and faculty held true to the vision that mind and spirit could be shaped and developed in a Christian context. By 1939 the college was positioned for growth as perhaps it had never been in its history. Graduating 26 students in 1938, Whitworth still appeared to have a long way to go to achieve stability. Yet in light of the fact that only 76 students had graduated from 1919 to 1929, Whitworth did seem to be entering a new era.

Ward Sullivan had provided needed leadership and stability at a crucial point in the college's history. The graduates from the '30s on would provide the basis for alumni support in years ahead. More importantly, a legacy of gritty determination had been established for future generations — a legacy upon which Frank Warren would build during the next generation.

Chapter VI - The 1940s

Building A Dream

*A*s isolated as north Spokane may have seemed from Oahu, Hickam Field, and Pearl Harbor, Whitworth was changed on December 7, 1941. "The majority of us stand behind President Roosevelt," *The Whitworthian* editorialized. "We believe that Japan has violated international law and Christian ethics by suddenly and deliberately attacking United States possessions while at the same time professing to want peace .... We are fighting against those forces of treachery which are opposed to the Christian way of life and to Christ's teaching of love and respect for all men, whatever their race may be."

The Whitworthian reported several alumni called to active duty, including Ralph Goodsell, Chaplain Frank Tiffany, Clemens Yeakel, and Lieutenant Lester Hansen. The feeling that everyone must aid the war effort permeated the campus. Within two months, faculty had established committees to build campus morale and to look at possible changes in the curriculum to increase its relevancy to the needs of the war. They added courses in aeronautics, pre-engineering and medicine.

The student newspaper ran advertisements reminding everyone to buy war bonds. College publications proclaimed that since its beginning, Whitworth had stood as "a bulwark for West-

Below - President Frank Warren (1940-1963): The longest tenure in Whitworth's history

Top - Chapel service in 1942

Bottom - Board of Trustees, 1946

ern Democracy." The new dean of the faculty, Merton Munn, helped coordinate a flight school at Calkins Airfield where 90 potential flyers received initial training.

At the same time, the dean expressed concern about what he perceived to be a devil-may-care attitude among some of the students. Dean Munn warned students that a wartime philosophy of "grasping at the moment whatever life presents for fear there will not be another" was self-destructive, and he did everything he could to persuade them to

do otherwise.

In the midst of war concerns, religious activities intensified. Students actively participated in Christian Endeavor groups and the Inter-Varsity Christian Fellowship Conference. Whitworth sponsored an all-city youth rally in 1942. Spiritual Emphasis Week focused attention on religious concerns, and student editorials called for more Christ-centeredness. The Whitworth community came together for chapel services three times a week. During the decade, countless speakers of

Above - *1945 faculty portrait*

Left - *Students and faculty dined together in McMillan until Leavitt Dining Hall was completed in 1944*

national stature came to Whitworth, including the evangelist Gypsy Smith and W. L. Young, president of Park College.

Perhaps this intensification had to do with the search for secure moorings in a stressful time, but it also had to do with the influence of Whitworth's new leader. On April 1, 1940, Whitworth's Board of Trustees selected a new president—the Reverend Frank Furniss Warren. Warren, who was to remain in office from 1940 to 1963, provided stability and leadership that would shape Whitworth for decades to come.

Warren, a graduate of Seattle Pacific College, studied at New York Biblical Seminary and Drew University. For three years in the 1920s, he served at mission stations in Osaka, Japan, and taught at the Osaka Biblical Seminary. He returned to Seattle Pacific in 1932 to serve as dean.

From the beginning, President Warren, a Free Methodist, sought to identify the college with a conservative theological position. He hired evangelical Christian faculty and focused his efforts

on the development of a liberal arts program with religious studies as an integral part. In his view, every subject should be related to Christianity. Science was to have a proper but not dominant part in the curriculum.

Frank Warren envisioned what he called "a committed student body." For example, in the 1943 *Natsihi*, "The President's Message to Marching Youth" exhorted students to face "long months of rigorous training, bitter hardship and personal sacrifice . . . that there may come back again a world of peace and kindness, brotherhood and love."

Never apologetic about required chapel and religious conferences, Warren frequently urged his faculty to demonstrate their concern for the spiritual condition of their students. The influence of Warren's infectious enthusiasm and deep commitment to the life of the college can hardly be overestimated.

Among Warren's most important faculty appointments in this era were three people in the religion and philosophy area. Mark Koehler returned to campus in 1942 to teach Bible. Students often affectionately referred to his classes as the "Gospel according to Mark." Joining him in 1944 was Evelyn Smith, who taught in the department until 1981. Professor Smith's many contributions were recognized when she received the Distinguished Lay Leader Award in 1989 from Whitworth President Arthur De Jong. Smith

and Koehler were joined in 1948 by Professor Larry Yates, who taught philosophy and Greek for 33 years.

John Koehler, Mark's brother, joined the faculty in 1945, beginning 30 years of leadership in art. On his retirement, his colleagues named the college art gallery after him.

Soon after coming to the Spokane campus, Warren realized that the facilities would have to be greatly expanded if Whitworth were to be competitive with other institutions. By late 1940, Warren had determined that the campus needed a gymnasium, an auditorium, a classroom building, a central heating plant, a men's dormitory, and a library. For the next two decades, Warren worked tirelessly to achieve these goals.

Replacing the old gymnasium was a top priority. Yet, just as plans were completed and construction about to begin, the United States found itself at war. Many materials, including metals, were in short supply because of the war effort. Not to be denied, Warren secured nails wherever he could, sometimes a handful at a time. He reserved a carload of concrete just before the government issued a freeze order, and the project began. All did not proceed without incident, however.

As the gymnasium site was being excavated, workers found a rock with a message in the form of unusual markings,

"10 day sence Vige John has feaver 1703." Word of the discovery spread quickly, along with speculation about its origins. When it became evident that media and outside experts were taking this seriously, student Sydney Eaton announced that the message was a hoax.

Students organized schemes to raise money, including a "Brickskrieg" which raised $3100 for bricks, mostly from downtown merchants. Although still unfinished, the building was the site of the 1942 Commencement. It was named Jay P. Graves Gymnasium, in honor of the trustee who had given the campus to the college.

The war, by reducing the student-age population, took its toll on colleges, Spokane Junior College among them. In 1941, SJC held its classes on the Whitworth campus. In 1942, Whitworth absorbed SJC's student body and some faculty, including its president, Gustav Schlauch, who was hired as a professor and became a great favorite among students.

The wartime internment of Japanese-Americans who lived on the U.S. Pacific coast also resulted in additions to the student body. As Japanese-Americans fled the coast, many moved in with relatives in Spokane rather than go to internment camps. Several became students at Whitworth. In 1944, ten percent of the student body was Japanese-Ameri-

Above - Biology Lab: Homer Alder leads science students through a cat dissection

Facing Page, Top Left Under construction: Graves gym in 1942

Facing Page, Lower Left - Syd Eaton and his "hoax" rock

Facing Page, Top Right - Building up Whitworth: Frank Warren transformed the campus with new structures and a strong spiritual dimension

Top - *This 1944 team included Japanese-American students who settled in Spokane to escape internment*

Above - *Shining Star: Sociology professor Gus Schlauch (l) was popular with Whitworth students*

can, including nearly half of the basketball team.

Whitworth had relatively few students when the war ended. Then came the G.I. Bill, and like most colleges and universities around the county, Whitworth greeted an onslaught of returning soldiers, eager to get an education and return to normal life. Enrollment climbed to record levels in the fall of 1945 and continued to increase for several years.

The most pressing problem was the need for more classrooms. Warren learned that government surplus buildings were available through the Mead Act, and in the next two years, he acquired ten buildings from Baxter General Hospital in Spokane and six from Port Orchard. While it was an inexpensive way to meet the sudden need for space, the buildings did nothing to improve the appearance of the campus. Nonetheless, many of them have been serving for nearly fifty years.

Grieve, Lancaster, Goodsell, Lincoln, and Nason Halls were among these buildings. Ralph Goodsell and Donald Lancaster were both killed in military service. Dr. and Mrs. Robert Grieve, missionaries, died in Ethiopia. Nason Hall was named after Blanche Nason, for her missionary work in Valdez, Alaska.

The post-war student influx also created an immediate need for married student housing. Twenty-two apartments were built from government surplus buildings. The dusty road past these quarters acquired the name "Ball and Chain Lane." Another government building provided two faculty apartments, although it contained design limitations since the building had served as a military stockade during the war.

The surplus buildings did provide

Whitworthian

VOL. 34   Spokane, Washington, Wednesday, November 25, 1942   NUMBER 2

BUILDER PRESIDENT'S GOAL IN SIGHT

'Building to Serve' Will Be Theme of 1942-1943 Natsihi

Editor Eleanor Hook Announces Appointment of Yearbook Staff Members

Regarding the completion in 1942-1943 of the Jay P. Graves auditorium-gymnasium as a happy symbol of the spirit of a college which seeks in all its departments to build men and women for consecrated service in their chosen fields, this year's staff of the *Natsihi* has chosen as yearbook theme, "Building to Serve."

Editor Eleanor Hook, formerly editor of *Pilot*, yearbook of Lindbergh high school, Valleyford, and freshman staff member of the *Whitworthian*, has announced as her associate, Marjorie Klein, '45.

Other staff appointments announced by the editor are: Classes, Lorraine Kitt; Organizations, Virginia Hodge; Sports, Vince Gregg and Florence Reynolds; Art, Virginia Huffman; and Photography, Ellen Jones.

Dr. Kennedy is faculty editoral adviser and Professor Dizmang, the *Natsihi's* first faculty business adviser.

The student business manager has not yet been selected, nor has the music editor.

The *Natsihi* is published annually under the supervision of the junior class, from whose ranks the editor is chosen by the class executive council acting in conjunction with the faculty editorial adviser.

◆◆◆

PRE-MEDS NOW ADMITTED TO HOSPITAL AUTOPSIES

Members of the Pre-Med club are now taking turns in attending operations and autopsies at St. Luke's and the Deaconess hospitals. Those in charge of arrangements are: President Loren Gothberg, Gerry Dean and Ruth Huntley.

Members are also working on a Pre-Med library to be located in the Biology lab. Books will be donated by Pre-Med students and will be for the exclusive use of the club members.

'Professor Huntley Accounts for Axis Bias of Gremlins

Alas, the allies have another treacherous enemy to battle. Not only do we have the axis on our hands, but some very formidable, pixy-like creatures, called "Gremlins," the R.A.F. points out.

According to the R.A.F., practically all the Allies' aerial trouble can be attributed to the Gremlins. This includes iced wings, jammed machine guns, water in the fuel line, poor vision, and a host of other troubles which confront the air fighters.

Now, the question is: What causes these otherwise normal little fellows to be so hostile to our side of the fight? This question has given rise to a considerable amount of investigation in the biology department, and several of the students have been studying the physiology and anatomy of the Gremlins in an attempt to discover the fault. What is it that makes the Gremlins so decidedly anti-ally?

Jack Starrett has been carefully studying Gremlin embryos, but finds nothing out of the ordinary in this phase of the development of the Gremlin. Ruth Huntley, however, has arrived at a very logical conclusion which accounts for the well-marked Gremlin nastiness. "Professor" Huntley has deducted, and also illustrated in a diagram which is on the biology laboratory blackboard, that the Axis doctors have removed the "conscience bumps" from the heads of the Grem-

Continued on Page 3

Monday, November 23, was more than just a birthday for Dr. Frank F. Warren this year. It was also the occasion for thankfulness that financial requirements for fulfillment of plans for the Jay P. Graves auditorium-gymnasium had been fully met, and that now the road to completion by the end of 1942 is clear.

HUNTER PROVIDES FOR FEAST IN MEN'S DORM

The entrance door to Professor Stanley Newcomb's apartment opened slowly. A man stood facing the reception room of Whitworth Hall. He stepped out, p a u s e d dramatically. Three little words fell from his lips.

An ominous rumble was heard throughout the building. Almost simultaneously, twenty doors opened; students poured by two's into the cor-

Continued on Page 4

Basketball Season Will Open on New Gymnasium Floor

Jay P. Graves Hall to Be Scene of Hoopsters' Battle With Gonzaga

When Whitworth's hoopsters open this year's Homecoming program, Friday, December 4, they will join battle with the Gonzaga quint on the floor of the new gymnasium. Meeting an opposing team for the first time in Jay P. Graves hall, the Pirates in their crimson suits will be spurred to victory not only by the yells of their student supporters, but by the music of Byquist's recently-organized pep band.

Following the game, all will gather around to watch the kindling of the big bonfire built by the freshman class. It is rumored that although there is no official recognition of rivalry, the freshmen may find it necessary to protect their prize pyre against certain upper classmen avowedly set on prematurely igniting the heap.

The formal banquet will be held Saturday evening.

Still busy sending letters of notification to graduates is Mary Elaine Dugan, chairman of the Alumni committee, under whose surveillance are Ruth Barnes, Bob Blodgett, Jackie Davis, Marge Klein, Bob Lee and Dorothy Munce.

Virginia Hodge is chairman of the Program committee, her associates being Vernon Forkner, Quentin Leisher, Florence Reynolds and Bill Schlauch.

In charge of decorations is Dorothy Beggs and her committee members, Virginia Huffman, Eugenia Ivanhoff, Wilfred Landres, Bob Paeth, Marcia Parker and Isabelle McNeely.

◆◆◆

PIRETTES FACED WITH PRIORITY ON SWEATERS

Because of war priorities Whitworth's new Pirette members will either have to go without the traditional crimson and gray sweaters or will have to persuade senior members to sell theirs.

Also on the Pirette schedule and now under way is the rewriting of their Constitution.

Whitworthian Staff Will Sponsor College Rental Library Bookshelf

When Whitworth students return to college after the Christmas recess, they will find a new bookshelf in the library. Recognizing the importance of keeping in touch with the thought of the world of today, the *Whitworthian* has volunteered to purchase twenty-five books as nucleus of a rental library of current fiction and non-fiction. Books will be selected from titles suggested by students and faculty members. All suggested titles should be deposited in the box provided for their reception at the desk in the library, on or before December 1. No unsigned suggestions will be considered.

The *Whitworthian* proposes Russell Blankenship's *And There Were Men*, that "brilliant new book" in which the distinguished professor of American Literature at the University of Washington is said to offer "a true and vivid portrait of the most colorful, mysterious, and romantic corner of America—the Pacific Northwest."

Top - President Warren moved buildings from Baxter Hospital onto campus after the war

Bottom - Washington Hall (Calvin Hall) originally housed a civilian pilot training program

Facing Page, Top - Harriet Cheney Cowles Library: Finished in 1948 with a gift from publisher William H. Cowles Sr.

more adequate space for the Whitworth chemistry, biology and physics departments. Since the beginning of Whitworth's history, science labs had been in the basements of dormitories.

In 1947, Tiffany Memorial Chapel was completed and named after Army Chaplain Frank Tiffany, '29. Captured in the Philippines, Tiffany developed an underground network to acquire medicine and food for his fellow captives. He was killed when the prisoner-of-war ship he was on was torpedoed and sunk in 1944. His widow, Estella Tiffany, began teaching in the Department of Education at Whitworth in 1949. Eventually Tiffany

Chapel was incorporated into the new Whitworth Community Presbyterian Church.

The most important building added during the immediate post-war years was the library. The Harriet Cheney Cowles Memorial Library, dedicated in 1948, was the gift of Spokane publisher William H. Cowles Sr. in memory of his wife. This building marked the beginning of a long relationship between the Cowles family and the college.

After the war, more articles and editorials began to appear in the student newspaper regarding international affairs, and Whitworth students began to express their political opinions much more vigorously. For example, in 1948, students produced a show for the newly-established radio station entitled, "What can we do to win the peace by economic and social rehabilitation in Europe?"

Major speakers came to campus. Olympic star Jesse Owens spoke in Chapel in 1946 and presidential candidate Harold Stassen visited in 1948. Later Stassen returned to campus in 1956 to receive an honorary doctorate from Whitworth.

While most of Whitworth's traditions from the pre-war years remained intact, certain ones began to disappear. The traditional junior chase of the senior sneak faded away, followed by the demise of the senior sneak itself in the early '50s.

During the election of student body officers, tacticians and strategists promoted their candidates with novelties like all-day suckers and campaign literature dropped from an airplane. But the platforms would not be unfamiliar to Whitworth students of any generation; planks focused on making Whitworth the best Christian college in the West, developing more cooperation among campus organizations, building more facilities for relaxation and study, improving bus service, and boosting athletics.

The campus election of 1948 symbolized some of the changes taking place. Among four candidates for president, two were veterans. One of those, Willis Case, had served four years in the Navy and survived the sinking of two ships. The eventual winner, Len Watson, was a veteran of the Coast Guard, married and the father of two children.

Student organizations emerged stronger than ever after the war. Student handbooks from the period provide a detailed listing of everything from the "W" Club for lettermen and the Intercollegiate Knights National Service Fraternity to Alpha Psi Omega for thespians; Phi Kappa Delta for debaters; Pirettes, Sefelo for all women in dormitories; the Modern Language Clubs; Alpha Kappa Chi for town students; and the Philadelphians, a group for young men preparing for full-time ministry.

Previous Page - *In the fast lane: Roller skating was the rage in the late 1940s*

Above - *McMillan Hall reception room*

Right - *A 1945 typing class*

Facing Page, Top - *Coronation: Culmination of the mid-winter Snow Frolic after a day on Mt. Spokane*

Facing Page, Bottom *Graves commons: A busy lunch spot in the basement of the gym*

Social events in the '40s included the Kampus Kapers Variety show, spring carnivals, an amateur hour and box social, auction of faculty members, and a Truth or Consequences show.

Freshman initiation still involved making students wear green ribbons, name tags, and frosh caps. Students had to act as shoe-shine boys, carry bags of foodstuffs, put books in wastepaper baskets, and walk on four-foot poles. The women had to wear their hair in pin curls, and the men had to wear feminine costumes. Conversation with the opposite sex was strictly forbidden for all freshmen, according to *The Whitworthian*.

Each year the Frosh-Sophomore tug of war ended with the losing class getting dunked in the Little Spokane River.

The annual Snow Frolic began in 1948 and survived into the early 1960s. Originally, professors dismissed all classes at 10 a.m. and students headed for the

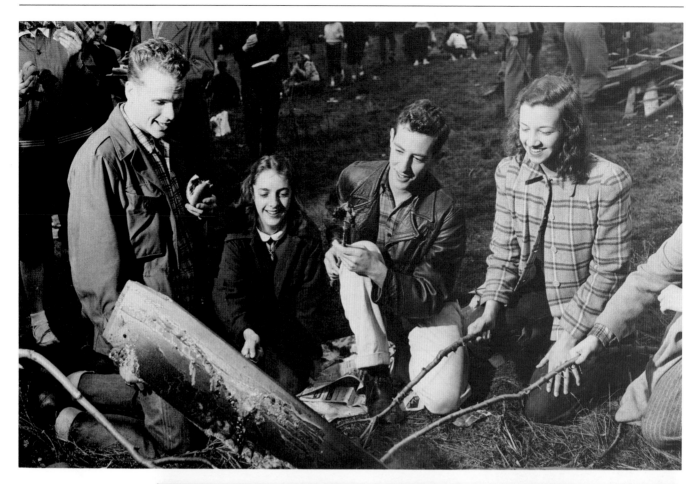

Above - *Wiener roast:
A Campus Day
tradition during the
1940s*

Right - *Winners of the
"Beard Contest," 1948.
L-R, Tex Clark,
Professor John Carlson,
Scott McClenny, Ray
Gouldin*

lodge on Mt. Spokane, where the event culminated with the crowning of a Snow Frolic King and Queen. Eventually the Frolic was moved to a weekend, but Kings and Queens reigned over winter fun for another fifteen years.

Even though many traditions remained and student activities proliferated, pressure mounted for a place to socialize on campus. When Graves Gym-

nasium was finished, part of the basement became known as the "Commons." For the first time, students could gather on campus for a milkshake or a coke. One writer in *The Whitworthian* described the Commons as a place where "the blues could be vigorously slammed in the corner in some other manner than 'kicking the bark off Whitworth pine trees.'"

But almost from the beginning,

Left - Women's
athletics in 1941

Below - Football team
of 1947

the Commons evoked student criticism. It was overcrowded during lunch, and heavy use took a toll on the condition of benches and booths. There were complaints about noise during Chapel, which was held upstairs in the gym. Finally the Commons was locked for the hour. "Surely no one ought to be pounding out 'Boogie-Woogie' when a chapel service is in session," the March 19, 1948 *Whitworthian* editorialized. "But if students have no place to congregate, they will be tramping up and down the stairs looking for a place to 'wait out' chapel."

Pranks and occasional vandalism marked the post-war years. By the late '40s, spiriting the silverware away from the dining hall on Halloween was a well-established tradition. One year, the silverware found its way onto a bus bound for Seattle—fortunately there was a return address. The number of missing items tended to grow each year, and President Warren pleaded with students to curtail the mischief. Trays disappeared from the cafeteria, and on one occasion all of the

Above - Pirate
basketball team
1947-48

Right - Spreading the
word: The campus
bulletin board

reference shelves in the library were emptied. The books had been neatly stacked on the counter and tables throughout the library.

After the war, basketball and football gained strength at Whitworth. After serving his country in the war, Jerry Stannard returned to Whitworth in 1946 and coached baseball, basketball, and football. Visiting basketball teams hated to play in the small confines of Graves Gym where the Whitworth student body sat close to the court. Earl Mortlock, a Whitworth favorite known as the "diminutive Pirate flash," and brothers Gerry and Jack Mahaffey led Whitworth to many victories in the late '40s. Bill Roffler and Clyde Matters, who later taught in the Education Department at Whitworth and subsequently became the president of Hastings College in Nebraska, were named to All-Conference teams.

Outstanding football players of the 1940s included Nick Faber, now professor of education at Whitworth, who was named All-Conference and Most Inspirational in 1949; Bruce McCullough; Vern Tucker, who was named in 1947 to All-Conference and All-Coast teams; and Sam Adams, who led the nation's small colleges in touchdown receptions in 1948. A Little All-American, Adams set NAIA career records by catching 120 passes for 2,191 yards and 25 touchdowns. As a freshman he set a NAIA record by catching nine touchdown passes in a single season. After several years in the pros, Adams returned in 1957 to coach the Pirates in

track. He took over football in 1958.

School rivalries flourished, especially against Eastern Washington and Pacific Lutheran. Central and Western Washington State Colleges, the College of Puget Sound, and St. Martin's College also were in the Evergreen Conference which Whitworth joined in 1948.

The decade ended with growing expectation that Whitworth would become the major Presbyterian institution in the Northwest, if not the entire West. Enrollment was up, new buildings reshaped the campus, and new faculty enriched the college's intellectual life.

But beneath the surface, seeds of tension were germinating as young people grew restless under the restrictions on social behavior that had been the norm at schools like Whitworth for so many years. A new understanding of what it means to be a Christian liberal arts college would evolve over the next forty years.

Top - Choir and director Wilbur Anders: Known for their a cappella style

Bottom - Start 'er up: Whitworth men proudly display their wheels

CHAPTER VII - THE 1950S

GLORY DAYS

The 1950s were good years for Whitworth. More students enrolled, major buildings were constructed, and the leadership of Frank Warren provided a steadying course for the college. The dream of educating both heart and mind flourished. The G.I. Bill enabled more students to attend college than ever before, and with America's unparalleled prosperity came a new mood of optimism and freedom. As the decade wore on, however, students found in heroes such as James Dean, Marlon Brando, and Elvis Presley reason to question the traditional values of their parents.

Like most Americans during the early '50s, Whitworth students hoped for a society free from war and from the Depression hardships their parents had endured. When the 1954 Supreme Court decision, Brown vs. Board of Education, declared that the concept of "separate but equal" discriminated against blacks, editorials and news articles in *The Whitworthian* showed growing awareness of civil rights issues.

During the Korean War, Whitworth students frequently expressed their opinions in the student newspaper regarding all kinds of world issues such as the firing of Douglas MacArthur and the plight of Korean children orphaned by the war.

When more international students

Facing Page - *Losing battle: Tug of war during freshman initiation*

Below - *McMillan Hall on a winter evening*

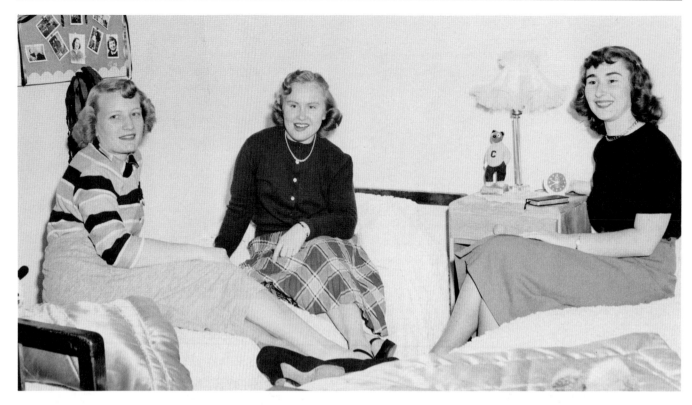

Top - *The college look: Curls, pearls, skirt and sweater were the style of the 1950s*

Bottom - *Snow frolicking on Mount Spokane*

began to come to Whitworth, they influenced the cultural atmosphere of the campus and made the Cosmopolitan Club one of the strongest student organizations. Designed to give support to non-American students, the club hosted social events, sponsored speakers, and promoted cultural awareness for Whitworth students. Officers in the '50s included Mike Maeda from Japan, Saisuree Vatcharakiet from Thailand (who would later be the first woman from her country to earn a Ph. D., and in 1988 would be selected to give the commencement address to Whitworth graduates), Eugenia Kim from Korea, Jim Wainaina from Kenya, Sadako Kurisaka from Japan, and Henry Fawcett from Alaska.

Political leaders came to speak on campus during this period, including Congressman Walter Judd of Minnesota in 1950, and Washington Governor Arthur Langlie in 1953. Polls showed Whitworth students usually preferred Republican candidates. In 1948, 64 percent of Whitworth students were for Thomas Dewey for president, while 20 percent were for Harry Truman; Whitworth faculty were 82 percent for Dewey, 9 percent each for Truman and Wallace. In 1952, a pre-election poll revealed that Whitworth students preferred Dwight Eisenhower 78 to 22 percent over Adlai Stevenson.

The late '40s and early '50s provided new consumer and entertainment opportunities. *The Whitworthian* ran regular articles and photographs describing the latest in fashions. "Sloppy Joes have gone their way," said an article in 1949. "Smarter Janes are now wearing the close-knit, short-sleeved slip-on. Add a string of pearls or a Peter Pan collar, and you have an unbeatable classroom attire."

Campus queen coronations for Snow Frolic and May Festival highlighted the social calendar. The Colonial Dance endured, sponsored by the Whitworth alumni association. In 1950, judges Larry Doyle from KGA, Dorothy Powers from the *Spokesman Review,* and Bob Johnson from the *Chronicle* selected Queen Janie Rebecca Williams.

"The queen wore a Colonial gown of white lace over a billowing crinoline skirt. The coat-type bodice was of gold

brocade, and she carried an arm bouquet of American Beauty roses tied with red satin ribbon. Queen Janie was finally presented gifts donated by downtown merchants."—*Whitworthian*, February 3, 1950.

Soon after, the Colonial, one of the longest of Whitworth's traditions, faded out of existence.

The May Festival continued to be popular early in the decade. Extending back to virtually the beginning of the college's history, this event had centered around the selection of a queen and her court. By the end of the decade, it too had lost some of its luster.

Homecoming also had a coronation, along with football games, pep rallies, "tire fires," and torchlight parades. In 1954, the Freshman Bonfire consumed 160 rubber tires, several apple trees, and a carload of railroad ties. On Friday night a torchlight parade wound through downtown, with the queen and her court in convertibles, followed by torch bearers, the school band and cheerleaders. The procession stopped for a pep rally at Howard and Sprague. On Saturday morning there was a campus parade of floats built by the dorms, decorated cars, and the John Rogers High School Band.

Top - *Queen Carol Siler is escorted by Dave Crossley at May Day 1955; Bill Rusk, in left foreground, returned to serve as financial aid director, 1968-1989*

Lower Left - *Hayride: A popular student outing*

Lower Right - *Cupid and Psyche at May Day Festivities*

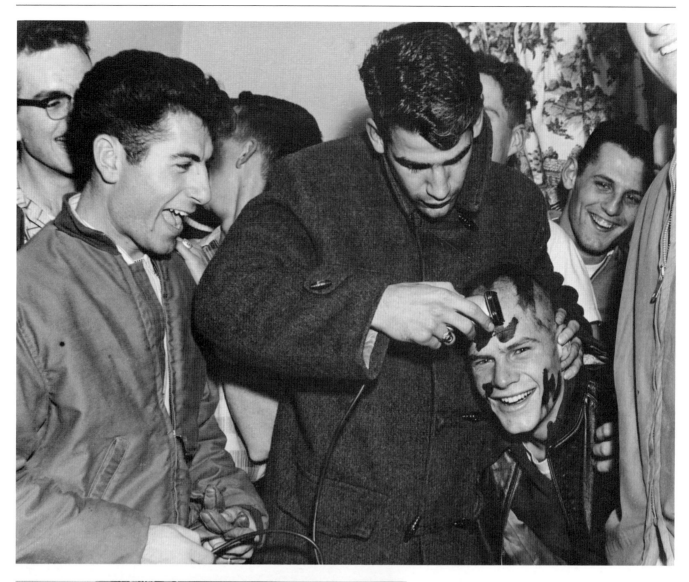

Top - *Gonzaga invader and Whitworth barbers*

Bottom - *Cheerleaders at a 1950s pep rally*

School spirit reached its zenith in the rivalries between Whitworth, Gonzaga, and Eastern Washington State College in Cheney. Students would sneak onto the other campuses and paint school letters on sidewalks, walls, or monuments. If caught, the invaders risked having the opposing school letters shaved into their heads. A victory bell was stolen so often that no one knows which school was the original owner. In 1950, school leaders and administrators attempted to institutionalize and control these rivalries by initiating joint pep rallies. Opposing students came to each other's campuses for yell-off competitions, but the idea was short-lived. Pranks were more fun!

Always eager to see the humorous side of their professors, students loved a revue called "Faculty Foibles." Dr. Warren sang famous old songs of Scotch comedian Harry Lauder. Mrs. Aaron Rempel and her "Twirling Baton" performed, followed by the Stomach Bucket Quartet — John Koehler, John Bachman, Bruce McCullough, and Coach Aaron Rempel — whose showstopper was "By the Sea." Fenton Duvall rendered cowboy music and Professor John Robbins performed a violin solo. The ever-popular Masters of Ceremonies were Dr. Theron Maxson and Professor John Bachman.

At Christmas, Hanging of the Greens included a banquet, carolling, a coed style show and the decoration of buildings throughout campus. The celebration of Christmas became in important event at the college; in the 1980s, alumna Gail Fielding played a major role in organizing the festivities and keeping alive the traditions that had been established by previous generations.

Romance on campus was always a lively topic of conversation. When a Whitworth couple became engaged, the traditional place for proposal was the "Whitworth Tree." This particular pine, located in the woods on the northeast side of campus, was uniquely curved to allow the young couple to sit together. Nevertheless, at least some students began to observe that this hallowed place was losing its revered position. "There was a time when every male on campus would shake in his boots at the mention of this botanical terror. Ask any coed on campus that has made the pilgrimage with her man. She will tell you the Tree has lost its spell, along with its comfort. A good project of the senior class could be to chop it down, as a remembrance gift. If you want to become engaged, follow the crowd to Warren Hall Lounge, the barbecue pit, or

Top - *Washington Hall serenades Ballard Hall after an engagement announcement at dorm devotions (1957)*

Above - *Off to the HUB for a study break*

Left - *The Whitworth Tree: Traditional place for romance to blossom*

perhaps the baseball dugouts. There is where romance blooms." *Whitworthian*, May 6, 1955

In those days, women's dorms had a ritual for engagement announcements. The residents would assemble in the lounge after 10 p.m. curfew. With the lights out, they'd pass a lighted candle from hand to hand until the betrothed blew it out, signalling the happy news. With a great shriek, everyone would express delight at the news and admiration of the engagement ring. Next day, in the dorm foyer, the bride-to-be would display the couple's portrait and names along with a dish of candy for everyone to enjoy.

Despite the frequency of engagement announcements on campus, complaints about dating, or lack thereof, surfaced frequently during the decade. Women students often accused the men of not doing their part socially. One tongue-in-cheek attempt at dating was the "One-Date-a-Month Club Fraternal Order" chartered in the mid-'50s. The rules: 1) No more than one "big" date (expenses not to exceed $5) a month; 2) total monthly expenses for casual dates, quantity unlimited, $2.50 or less, with a 50-cent maximum for any one date; and 3) a man may not date the same woman more than three times in a row without taking out another woman. "Non-adherents to the above rules," said the by-laws of the order, "along with irregular attenders at meetings, are subject to fines by the club treasurer. Every member of ODM is an officer." Tolo Week allowed women to ask men out on a date

as did the Sadie Hawkins-Dogpatch banquet. Couples vied for prizes with their Li'l Abner and Daisy Mae costumes. But the dating problem persisted. Even President Warren occasionally urged men on campus to make more effort to socialize with Whitworth women.

Compared to later generations, the students of the 1950s reflected conservative values and developed exceptional loyalty to the college. Yet the post-war student grew bolder in challenging some of the college's traditions and institutions. This took a certain amount of courage under Dr. Warren's administration. For example, the student newspaper frequently discussed the quality of the chapel programs. "With the planned reorganization, the 'good' Chapels could be sprinkled throughout the year so that the favorite speakers would pull the 'wanderers' back into the pattern," advised a 1957 editorial (February 15, 1957). Students talked about alternatives to mandatory attendance more and more frequently.

Dormitory regulations were another point of contention beginning in the 1950s. The house rules in McMillan and Ballard (both women's residences) forbade men to enter except during specific hours, and women were prohibited from leaving the dorm after 10:00 p.m. on weeknights. Men complained that they had to stand in the rain waiting for women to come down to meet them for a date.

Students also began to challenge the dress code that required men to wear ties and women to wear nylon stockings and dress shoes to dinner. The traditional family-style dinner would eventually fall under the pressure of student criticism. But through most of the decade, each woman, properly dressed for dinner, would file in to stand at every other chair and wait for the excruciating moment when a male student would deign to select a place next to her. After grace, the male would dutifully help his dinner partner be seated. The man at the head of the table paternally presided, dishing up food on the stack of plates before him. Quaint as it seems to the late twentieth century, the tradition fostered an intimacy that was lost when all meals became cafeteria style.

Square dances — "folk games" — were an attempt to satisfy the urge to

dance in the late '50s, but weren't enough. Student editorials frequently called for more social events. In 1954, movies received several trial runs before finally being approved permanently as part of the campus social scene.

What '50s students were interested in was varsity sports. It was an era when Whitworth was known throughout the region for its basketball and football. During the '50-'51 season, under Coach James McGregor, Whitworth's basketball fortunes began to climb with the skills of 6' 8" Ralph Polson, who would later play in the NBA. The highlight of the season was the defeat of then-undefeated Eastern Washington at Cheney, 75-60.

In 1952, Whitworth won conference and district playoffs, defeating P.L.U. and Gonzaga. At nationals, the Pirates defeated Wisconsin State Teachers' and James Millikin College before losing to Murray State in the quarter finals.

In 1954, under Coach Art Smith, Pirate players Ray and Roy Beach, Phil Jordan, Dave Eickerman and Wayne Hintz

Facing Page, Top -
Women's conferences and Spiritual Emphasis Weeks were regular events

Facing Page, Center -
"Men in the dorm!":
From the 1956 Natsihi

Facing Page, Bottom
Hawaiian Express: Basketball team takes off for a tropical tour

Above - Basketball duels drew big crowds in the 1950s and early 60s

Above - Jump ball: Women's basketball game from 1950-'51 season

Right - Nick Faber (later professor of education) in football stance

Below - It's a man's sport: The '55 Pirates charge through the slush in a 20-0 shutout of Montana State

led Whitworth to the conference championship and another trip to the NAIA championship. Jordan, 6'10", was an All-Conference center and a future NBA player. Unfortunately, Whitworth lost its first tournament game to Nebraska Wesleyan, 58-54.

In 1956, for the third time in four years, Whitworth went to nationals after defeating Gonzaga in a three-game play-off at the Spokane Coliseum. Ron Mill, Ralph Bohannon, Marv Adams, Dave Martin, Jack Thiessen, Fred Bronkema, Al Koetje, Max Sinn, Bob Gray and Dave Wackerbarth all made the trip to Kansas City, but Beloit, Wisconsin eliminated the Bucs in the first round, 88-75.

During the mid-'50s Whitworth upset Washington State University on a number of occasions. Art Smith, in three years as coach, won 41 of 48 conference games and 60 of 82 overall. Pirates named All-American included Polson, Jordan, Jim Doherty, Ray Washburn, Jay Jackson, and Ed Hagen.

Beginning in the late '40s under coach and future president of the college Mark Koehler, the men's tennis team established a tradition of success which continued under Clyde Matters who coached championship teams in 1949, 1950, 1955, and 1956. Coach Alvin Quall directed the team to the title in 1958 as did Coach Ross Cutter in 1959 and 1960.

Football at Whitworth reached its highest success during the mid-'50s. Beginning with the last game of the 1953 season and extending through the first two games of 1956, Whitworth won 20 consecutive games under coach Jim Lounsberry. Outstanding players included Wayne Buchert, Bob Bradner, Bob Ward, William Cole and Larry Paradis — all of whom were All-Conference and Little All-American award winners.

The mid-'50s were prodigious years for campus construction. McEachran Hall (named after Chairman of the Board William McEachran, 1923-1959), the administrative office building, was dedicated in 1952, and Dixon Hall (named after long-time trustee, Grant Dixon, Sr.) became the main classroom building in autumn 1956. President Warren had long sought an auditorium for chapel, drama events, concerts, and convocations. The Cowles family responded again with a major gift, and the auditorium was dedicated in February 1956. On February 20, chapel moved from Graves Gym to the new auditorium. Bleachers had not been the most

conducive environment for religious services, and the change caused great rejoicing.

Student handbooks in the late '40s promised that construction would soon begin on a new union building. But serious efforts to raise the money for the new student center did not begin until the early '50s. An attempt to secure a government loan had proved unsuccessful.

By November 1953, the total amount set aside for the building, which would be named in memory of Dean Francis T. Hardwick, was $30,000. A great deal of money still needed to be raised. The responsibility now rested largely with those who would benefit from the new building—the students.

Late in 1953, students divided themselves into what they called "HUB squads." These groups consisted of four members within a dorm. Contacting hundreds of potential contributors, each student canvassed the community with letters asking for support. Each letter contained an illustrated brochure describing the heritage and vision of the college. Despite the goal of $500 per squad, the

Above Left - One way: A sign in the snowy woods

Above Right - The Campanile Tower was built in 1956

Top Left - *Bribes and threats: Students cajole passerby to attend Varsity Variety show in Spokane*

Top Right - *Chaplain David Dilworth also headed the Bible Department*

Bottom - *Behind the eight ball: Students gather around a pool table*

success of this drive was marginal.

In February 1954, the faculty and dormitories sponsored a Mardi Gras in Graves Gym to benefit the HUB fund. A shoeshine booth staffed by faculty members, a jail, a cakewalk and many other carnival booths and games amused and entertained the crowd. The popularity of the Mardi Gras would lead it to become an annual date on the social calendar. The faculty dedicated proceeds from its "Faculty Foibles" to the HUB fund, and other similar shows put on both by students and faculty over the next few years benefitted the student union fund.

Then, in 1954, students tried a different approach—presenting the im-

portance of Whitworth College to Spokane businesses. Two hundred students underwent a salesmanship training program, then called on businesses, stressing the important cultural, religious, and athletic contributions that Whitworth provided to the community. At that time the college was spending about $1 million a year in the city. Nevertheless, more funds were still needed.

Student anticipation grew with the growing HUB fund. They accepted without complaint a tuition increase in 1955 that included a $7.50 assessment fee designated to the HUB fund. Administrators called the HUB project "the biggest student enterprise known to present genera-

tion Whits." The new building represented the third side of the "million dollar triangle" of Warren Hall and McEachran Hall.

Finally, in October 1955, plans were unveiled. They included a snack bar, dining room, banquet room, recreation room, lockers for town students, a barber shop, post office, offices of ASWC, and several lounges for both students and faculty. Planners discarded an original location behind Warren Hall because of its lack of visibility. The east end site, where the HUB stands today, provided a more central location. The plan also included a campanile in the center of the loop.

Fund-raising efforts alone could not raise the amount necessary and officials sought a government loan. The college financed the loan at a low interest rate over a period of 40 years.

On November 2, 1956, students held a ground-breaking ceremony and the following July was set as the completion date. Dedicated during the 1957 Homecoming celebration, the Hardwick Union Building was christened with the theme, "constructed with steel, tempered with prayer, and purposed for fellowship."

Faculty members who joined the staff in the '50s were to have a major impact on the Whitworth community. Among these were Dr. Clarence J. Simpson, who came in 1953 to head the department of English. Simpson became a teaching legend in the '50s and '60s. Along with Dr. Fenton Duvall, who had joined the department of history in 1949, Professor Simpson added stability to the liberal arts core. The names of Simpson and Duvall would come to symbolize the best of Whitworth's teaching. Outstanding in the classroom, both gentlemen touched hundreds of students' lives in profound ways. In 1955, Dr. Homer Cunningham came to teach history, and shortly thereafter established an American Studies program. Professor Cunningham involved his students in both local and national politics. In that same year, the Reverend David Dilworth began serving as chaplain and professor of religion. Many alums speak with great affection of Reverend Dilworth. Dr. Pat MacDonald also joined the Whitworth faculty in 1955

Above - Professor Mark Lee holds a speech class outdoors

Facing Page, Bottom Right - Estella Baldwin (l), college registrar and Marion Jenkins (r), Dean of women

***Above** - Art professor
John Koehler at work*

in the department of psychology. She recalls that her first year's salary was $3,600. She began what would be one of the longest teaching careers in the history of Whitworth. An important influence on many Whitworth students, Professor MacDonald helped lead the way for other

female faculty members in subsequent decades. In 1990 she was still an active member, of the faculty as were Howard Redmond in religion (1957), Tom Tavener in music (1959), and Bob Bocksch in chemistry (1959). These three professors influenced countless students with their outstanding teaching.

Professor Redmond helped organize a faculty quartet in the late '50s and early '60s with Tom Tavener, Virgil Grieppe, and Milton Erway. While members changed (in the late '80s, members included Redmond, Frank Houser, Bob McCroskey, and Paul Olsen), the group performed at various functions for more than thirty years.

The Whitworth Choir, under the direction of Wilbur Anders, emerged as one of the most respected groups in the region. Mr. Anders taught at Whitworth from 1947-57 after studying under the famed director F. Melius Christiansen at St. Olaf College in Minnesota. Anders'

choirs, known for their a cappella style, received critical acclaim on their annual tours.

Drama continued to be an important student activity during the 1950s. Loyd Waltz directed many fine productions. In 1952, "St. Claudia" was performed on campus and starred Beverly Mumford, George Wheeler, and Weldon Ferry, among others. Spokane residents enjoyed productions such as "Everyman" in 1956, which starred Donn Crail, Richard Wright, and William Burd as the voice of God.

In these years, faculty strove to raise the level of academic excellence during the decade. In 1956, a journalism departmental honors program at Whitworth attracted the attention of Dean Alvin B. Quall. Two years later, an all-college Honors program came into being. Those juniors and seniors accepted for the program were challenged with more rigorous requirements, including a thesis, which the Honors student had to defend before the Honors Council. Most of the Honors graduates pursued graduate degrees after leaving Whitworth. The first to receive a Ph. D. was Joseph Powell,

who was commissioned to develop a department of marine biology at the University of Beirut in Lebanon.

The new prestige of the college was reflected in the fact that Whitworth, along with 125 other private colleges, made *Good Housekeeping*'s annual report. The only other Washington state college mentioned was Whitman. (*Whitworthian*, February 9, 1951)

Among the outstanding students of the decade was Dick Gray, winner of the first Danforth fellowship for journalism in the United States. He was also an All-American editor at Whitworth and president of the student body. After his untimely death, his peers called him one of the premier journalism educators in the United States for his work as the head of the School of Journalism at Indiana University.

As the decade ended, President Warren began to anticipate not only the 20th anniversary of his coming to Whitworth but also the 75th anniversary for the college in 1965. The decade had been good to the college. By 1949, 878 students had earned degrees from Whitworth. During the next ten years, from 1950-59, 1,503 people graduated from the college, nearly double all of the previous years combined. Enrollment continued to climb, new faculty had come, and major buildings had been constructed. And while students had more frequently questioned some of the practices of the college, all seemed well. Few, however, were prepared for the turmoil that would emerge during the decade to follow.

Facing Page, Top - Ball & Chain Lane: 40s and 50s Married student housing (Jerry Wilson family)

Above Left - Back to the future: Marilyn Ashburn and Bill Tatum in 1952 "Whitworth Capers"

Above Right - Whitworthian staff: Editor Dick Gray (center) surrounded by his fellow journalists

CHAPTER VIII - THE 1960S

CURRENTS OF CHANGE

*P*erhaps no other decade in American history is more associated with the college generation than is the 1960s. The word "sixties" has come to be almost synonymous with long hair, student protest, rioting, drugs, and sexual liberation. It is often difficult, even for those who lived through the period, to remember how relatively conservative students were during the first part of the decade. A glance at college annuals anywhere, let alone Whitworth, reveals short hair, school spirit, and genuine patriotism. Yet, as we have seen, several currents of change were in the air even as the decade of the '50s closed. Combined with the rising tide of the Civil Rights movement, the raised levels of consciousness about political issues expressed in folk and rock music, as well as the increasing feeling that something was going wrong in Vietnam, the Baby Boom generation of college students began in earnest to challenge traditional authority. By the end of the decade, Whitworth, like most institutions, had experienced a significant degree of change only hinted at in the beginning. Students asserted their rights, challenged professors, and rejected what they believed were tired traditions.

Faculty and students debated the nature of a liberal arts education and the role of Christianity in American culture. Few periods in American history have produced such ferment or been fraught with greater anxiety. Yet through it all,

Facing Page - *Varsity quartet: Don Hoff, Paul Dorpat, Eldon Blanford, Blair Patrick and Dave Lutz (not visible) at piano*

Below - *Future President: Young Democrats club brought John F. Kennedy to campus during his 1960 presidential campaign*

Above *-Whitworth Christian Fellowship advisors for 1961: (l to r) Frank Houser, Ella Erway, Evelyn Smith, Mae Whitten, Dave Dilworth and Harry Dixon*

Right *- Snow-Frolic Court of '63: (l to r) Joan Hansen, Dan Lazear, Carolyn Griffith, Roberta Poore, James Cole, Judy Margrath and Jack Shriver*

Whitworth remained a relatively safe place where young students could develop new world views.

Politics was a hot topic on campus when the youthful senator from Massachusetts, John F. Kennedy, came to Whitworth in February 1960 to address the students while he was running for president. President Warren could find only one avowed Democrat on the faculty, a young professor of sociology by the name of Frank Houser, to introduce the senator. Even Kennedy's personal appearance, however, could not persuade a majority of students to cast their votes for him in the campus election. In a poll shortly before the November contest, of 458 votes cast, 362 went for Nixon-Lodge and only 96 indicated a preference for Kennedy-Johnson. Shortly thereafter, students and faculty members began to shift allegiance away from the Republican party.

President Warren continued to be firm in his commitment to building an institution grounded in evangelical Christianity. He consistently upheld traditional rules and regulations on dorm life, dancing, smoking, drinking, and of course he argued for mandatory chapel.

Both the men's and women's conferences in the early '60s featured the Reverend Donn Moomaw, All-American

football player, pastor of First Presbyterian Church of Berkeley, California, and associate of Billy Graham.

Spiritual Emphasis Week speakers included the Reverend Bob Munger, pastor of South Hollywood Presbyterian Church, a specialist in college youth activities, and Dr. Louis Evans, one of the most widely known Presbyterian clergymen of the day.

These Spiritual Emphasis Weeks made dramatic impressions on many Whitworth students. Confronted with the challenge of commitment to Christ, students often came away from these events strengthened in their faith and renewed in their fellowship with faculty and fellow students.

Traditions remained strong early in the decade with such events as May Festival, Snow Frolic on Mount Spokane, Hanging of the Greens, and Belshazzar's Feast filling the campus calendar. Students took keen interest in selecting royalty candidates for Homecoming and other events, which reflected the importance of these campus activities in those years.

In 1960, the achievements of the

baseball team established a high point in the college's athletic history. That spring, Whitworth won the NAIA championship. The team was led by pitcher Ray Washburn, whose subsequent eight-year career with the St. Louis Cardinals included pitching a no-hitter. Walter "Spike" Grosvenor, now professor of art, was also one of the team's pitchers.

Top -Homecoming float

Bottom - 1961 Mardi Gras Homecoming Court: Queen Lois Burt with honor princesses Kathleen Jones (l) and Linda Devine

Above - *NAIA National Champions: The sluggers of 1960 were (l to r, top row) coach Paul Merkel, Bob Huber, Jerry Breymeyer, Ray Washburn, Ron Lince, assistant coach Ken Wittenberg, (middle row) Dean McGuire, Jim Glennon, Farrel Romig, Norm Harding, Dennis Reiger, Abe Roberts, (bottom row) Spike Grosvenor, Bill Roberts, Jerry McCracken, Don Cox, Lee Archer and Tom Ingram*

Right - *Sportsmen: (l to r) Football captain John Murio, baseball coach Paul Merkel and basketball captain Gary McGlocklin display trophy for sportsmanship awarded to Whitworth players and spectators for 1962-63 seasons*

The 1960 team started out slowly by losing the first two games to the University of Washington, but finished with a 16-7 record and the Evergreen Conference and NAIA district titles. In the national tournament, the Pirates won four of five games, defeating Georgia Southern 4-0 for the championship.

A police escort met the team on their return to Spokane for a celebration parade downtown before throngs of students and loyal supporters. This championship was the highlight of Coach Paul Merkel's career at Whitworth. An athlete during the '40s at the college, Merkel returned to Whitworth in 1954 to coach. Inducted into three separate sports halls of fame, Paul Merkel has had a positive influence on student athletes for more than thirty years.

The 1960 football team, directed by Sam Adams, also had an outstanding year. It was one of four teams selected to participate in the NAIA national playoffs, but lost 13-7 to Humboldt State College in the semi-finals.

Above Left - Coach Sam Adams with Whitworth record-holding running back Charlie Reed (34) and all-conference end Dave Morton (82)

Above Right - First at NAIA Districts, 12th at Nationals: 1967 cross country team with (top row) coach Arnie Pelluer, Loren Minnick, Monte Moore, Len Long, Bob Ensign, (bottom row) Earl Carrol, Larry Miller, Iain Fisher and Jerry Tighe

Lower Left - The wind-up: Fred Shaffer took NAIA discus championship in 1960

Lower Right - And the pitch: Ray Washburn led the Bucs to their 1960 NAIA title and went on to play for the St. Louis Cardinals

Outstanding football players in the decade included Ken Sugarman, Charlie Reed, who rushed for a school record 245 yards in a single game in 1962, and Larry Jacobson, who was named a Kodak All-American in 1968.

Sam Adams also developed an outstanding track and field program as well as nationally ranked cross-country teams. The 1964 and 1965 cross-country teams placed second in the NAIA national championship in Omaha. In 1966, the Pirates were ninth, and in 1967, twelfth. Adams' track teams won four Evergreen Conference titles during the late '50s and early '60s. Jim Klein was an alternate in the decathlon on the 1960 Olympic team, and Fred Shaffer set a national record in the discus, 185'1/3", in 1963. All efforts, however, did not end in glory; one person recalled the day when an athlete blacked out nine square miles of Spokane by throwing a javelin over the power lines near the baseball field.

Under Coach Dick Kamm, the Pirate basketball team made yet another trip to the national tournament in Kansas City in 1961 but again lost in the first game. John Utgaard and Ed Hagen led a series of strong teams in the early '60s. An 80-71 win in 1967 over rival Gonzaga was particularly satisfying, but overall success became more elusive as the decade progressed. The tennis team finished fourth in the NAIA tournament in 1961, and ninth in the country in 1966. For much of that time, the women's program

was led by Diana Marks, who had come to the college in 1956 to teach and coach.

Whitworth, like many college campuses in the early '60s, became infatuated with folk music. Numerous groups came to campus — the Highwaymen, the Wayfarers, the Serendipity Singers, and Glen Yarbrough. In 1963, students Vicki Sanders, Bill Johnson, and Bob Knowles won an audition contest when they appeared at a Northtown hootenanny, and RCA asked them to make an album.

The '60s found Whitworth graduating many fine students including English major Bob Duvall ('62), who became president of Pacific University in Forest Grove, Oregon, and Stephen Davis from the same class, who became a professor of philosophy at Claremont McKenna College. Tammy Reid graduated in 1960 and came back to Whitworth in 1971 to teach. In 1988, she became the Associate Dean of Academic Affairs for the college. A 1964 graduate, Sharon Parks became an Asso-

ciate Professor of Psychology at Harvard. Robert Clark graduated in 1967 and returned to Whitworth to teach sociology first in the early '70s and then again in 1987. Mike Goins graduated in 1968 and returned to serve as Vice-President for Business Affairs. A 1962 graduate, Rod Hansen returned to Whitworth in 1981 to teach mathematics.

In the midst of fairly serious academic pursuits, college pranks continued unabated, symbolizing the carefree environment of the early decade.

A Volkswagen appeared on the steps of McMillan porch at 2:00 a.m. A nocturnal race through the loop by several Volkswagens tested the resources of the one campus policeman. The men of Westminster Hall built a reputation for the most creative pranks, mainly on the strength of the Westminster "rails," old jalopies stripped of everything except the wheels, chassis, and gas tank. In leather helmets and goggles a la Barney Oldfield, they would race these jalopies around the

loop. When the administration banned them, the Westminster men, undaunted, raced their jalopies on a figure eight track where the fieldhouse now stands. The male students started another new tradition, the "senior ride." Graduating seniors were "kidnapped," often stripped of everything but their shorts, and dropped off somewhere in the surrounding countryside to make their way back to the campus on their own. One resourceful student found employment on a nearby farm for a few days and remained unaccounted for long enough to teach his captors a lesson. On another occasion, enterprising Westminster men actually excavated ground underneath the dormitory in order to create a private room. Westminster men would often plug up the drain in the shower and wait for some unsuspecting freshman to open the door.

In 1965, long before streaking was fashionable on college campuses, the Society of Streakers originated at Whitworth. These hardy men, suitably unattired, raced past the row of women's dormitories on snowy nights. To be in good standing, members were required to wear a single item, the group's "calling card"— a post-office logo of the naked, wing-footed silhouette of Mercury, Roman god of speed, cleverness, travel, and thievery. That winter, the number of streakers increased, as did the frequency of their efforts. Team-streaking became a dormitory event, and one group performed only to the tune of "The William Tell Overture." Finally the lone campus policeman was called upon to cover the situation and put an end to it.

Campus additions included the

Fieldhouse, a gift from Trustee C. Davis Weyerhaeuser; Arend and Stewart Halls; as well as the Eric Johnston Science Center. The Cowles Auditorium organ was installed in 1964, celebrated by several major concerts, including one by noted organist E. Power Biggs.

When asked to reflect on what it meant to live in the decade of the sixties, many Whitworth graduates begin with their memory of President Kennedy's assassination in November 1963, and the death of President Frank Warren less than a month later. The Kennedy death touched virtually all college students, because many at Whitworth recalled vivid memories of Kennedy's speech in Cowles Auditorium in February 1960. Warren, of course, had been responsible for the tremendous growth that had occurred in the post-World War II era. No other president in the history of the college had wielded such influence over the spirit of Whit-

Top - Women's intramural football (1964)

Bottom - Goodsell-Lancaster men charge to an intramural victory over the Westminster Hall team

Above - *Queen candidates with '63 football squad*

Right - *Solidarity: Some of the men of Westminster*

worth. In a very tangible way, the deaths of both Kennedy and Warren marked the passage into a new and perhaps less innocent period both for the United States and for the college.

President Warren had grown noticeably tired during the previous spring, and by September he was diagnosed with cancer. After giving the opening address of the school year, he entered the hospital the same day. Against doctor's orders, he mustered strength to speak briefly at the Homecoming Banquet in the Davenport Hotel. For most people, that was the last time they saw Dr. Warren alive. He continued to play a role in college decisions from his hospital room, and spent the evening before he died listening to a Whitworth basketball game. Messages from around the country eulogized him; few questioned that Whitworth had emerged as one of the preeminent Presbyterian institutions largely because of Frank Warren's vision and hard work.

Earlier, the Board of Trustees had named Dr. Mark Koehler as executive vice-president. On May 29, 1964, Koehler was selected president. A graduate of Whitworth, Dr. Koehler has been the only alumnus to serve as president. He had pastored several congregations before returning to Whitworth to head the Bible and Christian education program in 1943.

Mark Koehler took office with high hopes and great expectations; but the next few years, while rewarding in many respects, would be difficult, not only for Koehler but for almost every college president in the country.

President Koehler gave his support to faculty efforts to improve the curriculum. Dr. John A. La Coste, head of the department of Education, suggested several curriculum revisions and re-alignment of departments. Earlier, the Phi Beta Kappa faculty (William G. Wilson, Robert Bocksch, Nicolin Gray, James Wadsworth, and Alfred O. Gray) had been commissioned to determine whether Whitworth could successfully apply to be a chapter.

Washington University.

By the end of the decade, Lillian Whitehouse-Lyle began developing Whitworth's Continuing Education programs. Most notably, Ms. Lyle helped originate a program entitled "Women in Transition." Intended to enrich the lives of working women as well as those who had never earned a degree, "Women in Transition," under the direction of Elsa Distelhorst, continued to thrive through the '80s and symbolized Whitworth's commitment to the larger Spokane community.

In 1965, Dr. Koehler presided over the celebration of Whitworth's seventy-fifth anniversary. The gala year was highlighted by several special events including television personality Ralph Edwards hosting a "This is Your Life—Whitworth College." Included as participants were Mrs. Delores Peck, great-granddaughter of George Whitworth; Kenneth Ghormley, 1908 football star and Rhodes Scholar qualifier; and A.W. Carlson, one of the first students on the Spokane campus. The publication of Al Gray's *Not By Might*, the history of the college, also added much to the appreciation of Whitworth's heritage.

Student activism began at Whitworth, as it did on many campuses, as questions over students' rights and attitudes of rebellion arose with increasing frequency. But early in the decade, there was still a conservative twist to it. For example, in 1961, *The Whitworthian* ran a headline, "Students Rebel Against 'Illegal' Rule." Paul Gilberson, Bob Quall, and

Above Left - *President Mark L. Koehler (1964-1969): First Whitworth alum to lead the college*

Above Right - *President Frank Warren*

Lower Left - *Dean of the faculty, Dr. Clarence J. Simpson*

While not successful in securing a chapter, the committee made twenty-two recommendations to the administration for overall academic improvements. Dr. Koehler worked at these, making substantial progress in raising salaries, improving the library budget, and increasing endowment.

It was during this period that Whitworth began to develop its graduate program in Education, primarily under Dean Alvin Quall. From the mid-'60s on, Whitworth would graduate an average of 70 master's a year, primarily in Education. Dr. Quall also helped to initiate, in 1968, Whitworth's participation in the Intercollegiate Center for Nursing Education, a consortium involving Whitworth, Washington State University, and Eastern

Vern Visick donned arm bands and hats to protest the fact that the new ASWC constitution had not been approved by the faculty. These students argued that the student exec had misused executive power and that the constitution was illegal. By the end of the decade, it would have been a major victory to have passed a constitution *without* faculty approval.

In 1963, using the principle of the students' right to know, *The Whitworthian* successfully challenged the long-standing tradition of not publicly announcing vote totals for student body elections.

A more serious protest erupted in January 1964 over the quality of food on campus. Five male students picketed the college dining hall and set off a larger demonstration that included a march around the loop and a boycott of the evening meal. Terry Casteel, student body president, forcefully articulated students' concerns and the protest proved effective. The administration soon approved the hiring of SAGA Food Services.

In general, student activism had two targets: specific campus regulations and social issues in the world, particu-

larly the Civil Rights movement and the war in Vietnam.

Student editorials in the mid-'60s urged reconsideration of all traditions, especially campus beauty contests. Another sign of changing sexual attitudes was evident when necking in the dorm lounges became an issue in 1965. Many students believed in a strictly enforced prohibition of necking, while a growing number expressed belief that student freedom superceded the right of the college to regulate anything other than illegal behavior.

Dancing also was a major point of debate. In late 1965, a student poll revealed that 85 percent favored social dancing. As a result, the Student Senate unanimously passed a resolution recommending that the Board of Trustees make dancing part of Whitworth's program. "Dancing itself is not the major issue. Of far greater significance is the question of the college's position as legislator of Christian standards or morals," argued Skip Brown, *Whitworthian* editor. "Whitworth does seek to be a Christian institution but at a time when students are questioning values and their position as relating individuals in a greatly changing world,

Whitworth needs to re-evaluate her position in relation to legislative rules and Christianity." The Board of Trustees approved dancing at the next meeting, in February 1966. Skip Brown, after graduation, became a CBS-TV photojournalist with assignments in Vietnam and China.

The general concern over student rights led the Board of Trustees to pass a Student Bill of Rights in 1969 in order to guarantee freedom of speech in the classroom and freedom of student expression.

While many professors advocated political activism early in the decade, what they had in mind was something more orthodox than what developed later in the decade. The Model United Nations Conference in the spring of 1964 serves as the best example of this more mainstream approach. Led by student Bob Yearout and political studies professor Gus Haas, it was called the largest student project in Whitworth history. Over 1,200 students from 102 schools participated, representing 104 countries in the 14th session of the Model UN.

Classes were nearly empty that week as sessions were held on Whitworth's campus. Whitworth students served as pages, security guards, and executive

Above - Model United Nations: Whitworth hosted 1200 students from over 100 colleges for this 1964 event

members of committees. Major speakers from the U.N. spoke at the event.

Events occurred so rapidly in the decade, however, that students grew increasingly impatient with simply pursuing gradual change through institutions like the United Nations. Guest speakers on campus often raised social issues to a new level of discussion. One of them, Giovanni Costigan, University of Washington professor of history and an outspoken critic of U.S. foreign policy, addressed the students in 1963. Often accused of being sympathetic to communism, Costigan and others urged more social activism and openly criticized the "establishment." Activist William Stringfellow spoke during Spiritual Emphasis Week in 1966 concerning poverty, racism, and the Christian call to change the world. In other years, Spiritual Emphasis Week featured speakers on such controversial topics as LSD, sex, and war.

The war in Vietnam was extremely divisive for Whitworth students, as it was for the country as a whole. Whitworth students remained largely conservative, however, at least through 1968. Richard Nixon won campus elections in both 1960 and 1968, and while, nationally, Barry Goldwater lost to Lyndon Johnson, on the Whitworth campus in 1964 he had a very strong contingent of support. The Berkeley student riots received a significant amount of coverage in *The Whitworthian*. Nevertheless, as late as November 1967 (just prior to the Tet Offensive), Whitworth students supported American involvement in the war 310 to 148, although support for the draft was only 267 to 258.

Students established a draft counseling office in 1969 to provide information about their options. Poignant letters from Whitworth graduates serving in Vietnam appeared in *The Whitworthian*. In May 1969, Benjamin Spock, the baby doctor and anti-war activist, denounced the draft in a campus speech. Later that year, the student government endorsed participation in the nationwide Moratorium Day, October 15, in order to study war and its impact on the world.

But the issue that surfaced most prominently on campus during the '60s was racism, particularly the role of blacks—or lack thereof—at Whitworth.

Beginning in 1964, a handful of black students, as well as an increasing number of white students, began expressing opinions about whether prejudice existed on campus. Perhaps the most prominent black student was Eddie Matthews. Matthews not only was an outstanding athlete, but also played the title role in the theatre arts production of Othello, was a yell king, and served as president of the Associated Men's Student organization. In a *Whitworthian* in-

Above - *Othello: 1964 cast included Ed Matthews as Othello, Jim Grady as Cassio and Bruce Reid as Iago*

terview, Matthews said mostly favorable things about Whitworth, but said he believed he had only been selected for black acting roles and that in general Whitworth students were apathetic toward racism.

In 1966, James Farmer, the national secretary for the Congress of Racial Equality, spoke at Whitworth about black problems in America, and later, in a speech on campus, activist theologian William Stringfellow remarked about how few blacks were currently attending Whitworth. Concerned students began to apply increased pressure on the administration to explain why. In May 1968, an open student letter to "concerned parents" appeared in *The Whitworthian*: "Although you shouldn't expect to be held captive overnight in the ad building by local left-wingers, or to have your son busted for possession of pot, or even to have some zealous member of the God Squad press the Four Spiritual Laws on you, you should be briefed, as an interested party, on the actual state of affairs at Whitworth.

"Our student body is an interesting example of a trichotomy divided by ideas and action. There is that segment which possesses virtually no ideas and no action. Secondly, there is that part which has the right idea, but always seems to have a test to study for when action is needed. Finally, there is that minority which possesses both ideas and the willingness to act. This situation will confront anyone who has attempted to drag this student body, kicking and screaming into the twentieth century." *Whitworthian*, May 1968.

The writer pointed out that only four black students attended Whitworth in the 1967-68 school year, and proposed that the college undertake new recruiting efforts and offer more financial aid directly to blacks.

The Whitworth administration took this criticism to heart and embarked on the most ambitious recruitment of blacks in the college's history, in what was known as Project Opportunity. Admissions counselors sought students in New York City's Harlem, and by fall, nearly twenty blacks were registered to attend classes. Momentum toward more commitments to black students continued to build in fall 1968, when Civil Rights leader Julian Bond spoke in Chapel.

*Above - English
Professor: Leonard
Oakland stands before
his class in 1966*

"Whit Soul" column. Written by blacks, it offered them a forum for expression as well as a way to raise the consciousness of white students about black issues.

In many ways, the '60s marked an important transition for the college. The death of Frank Warren symbolized the passing of an era. The transition was emphasized in the retirements of Marion Jenkins in 1965 and Estella Baldwin in 1968. Marion Jenkins, dean of women and professor of religion, influenced hundreds of students during her 34 years at Whitworth (1931-1965). Upon retirement, she received the Whitworth Alumni Distinguished Service Award and the Board of Trustees awarded her an honorary doctorate. Estella Baldwin served from 1931-1968 and was registrar for 34 of those years. She too received the Whitworth Alumni Distinguished Service Award at her retirement.

New faculty took over. More than a dozen members of the faculty who would still be teaching at the centennial in 1990 began their tenure at Whitworth College during the '60s. These included Howard Gage in Mathematics (1969), Walter "Spike" Grosvenor in Art (1968), Pierrette Gustafson in French (1963), William Johnson in Psychology (1968), Leonard Oakland in English (1966), Pat Stien in Theatre Arts (1966), George Weber in Business (1965), and Shirley Richner in Education (1966), who later became the first woman to hold a vice-presidential position. In addition, George Ross in the department of music began a teaching career at the college that would span twenty-two years (1965-87).

The natural sciences were significantly strengthened with the addition of new faculty. Howard Stien (1965) and David Hicks (1967) came to teach biology with Nicolin Gray, who had come in 1956 and retired in 1980. Stien and Hicks were still teaching at the time of the centennial. In chemistry, Robert Bocksch had come in 1958 and was still heading the department in 1990; Hugh Johnston joined the chemistry faculty in 1957, and Robert Winniford (1963-1984) lent stability to the department. Geology Professor Edwin Olson came to Whitworth in 1960 and was still heading the department in 1990. Aided by the completion of the Eric Johnston Science Center in the fall of 1963,

Letters in the student newspaper reveal increased tension between white and black students and a willingness by black students to be vocal concerning their view of oppression.

Professor Lew Archer, then director of Project Opportunity, which included most of the black students, agreed to be advisor to black students and to help teach a January course on Afro-American History with history professor Homer Cunningham. The class, with 15 black and 115 white students, at times became extremely tense. Thirty guest speakers were invited; all were black. In 1969, a Black Student Union was established, and in April, black students picketed the administration building, charging that President Koehler had reneged on promises to hire a recruiter who could relate to non-white students and a black professor for a course in Afro-American history in the regular semester. A small number of white students counter-demonstrated.

The Whitworthian began to carry a

Left - Resident counselors for the women's dorms: (l to r) Ruby Williams, Rosa Cardwell, Helen Bailie, Sylvia Claytor, Martha Olson, Gladistine Mikesell and Eileen Hendrick

Below - Dining Hall dance: Ballard girl Vivian Hamilton and Rick Hornor (later Theatre Arts professor)

this core group of faculty produced an outstanding number of graduates who went on to success in a range of science fields.

In the spring of 1969, President Koehler announced his acceptance of a pastoral call. Under Koehler, Whitworth had experienced significant change. The 4-1-4 calendar, the core curriculum, expansion of the faculty, and the initial computerization of business records marked his administration. The campus saw the construction of major buildings including Stewart and Baldwin-Jenkins Halls, and a major addition to the Cowles Library. Yet the last few years of the decade proved very difficult for students, faculty, and administration.

Whitworth was not alone in its difficulty facing the perplexing ferment of the late '60s. Faculty were under pressure to make courses more relevant to issues ranging from foreign policy and civil rights to poverty and sexual discrimination. The administration also faced pressure from students, faculty, trustees, and parents both to change with the times and to uphold standards that were under serious attack. Most faculty, however, regard these years as a time in which energy and creativity ran high. But the national mood in 1969 was one of uncertainty. In part, this uncertainty led Whitworth to select for its next president someone who was as positive about the future as anyone in the country.

CHAPTER IX - THE 1970S

THE LINDAMAN ERA

*O*n May 4, 1970, national guardsmen fired shots at anti-war protesters and killed four students at Kent State University in Ohio. College students across the country, in shock and rage, took to the streets in some of the largest protests of the anti-war movement. At Whitworth, 350 students, nearly one quarter of the student body, gathered in the Loop and listened for three hours as speakers condemned American policy in Vietnam and lamented the deaths of the four students. Several Whitworth students fasted in front of the administration building and demanded that the college publicly criticize American policy and terminate relations with the R.O.T.C. The agonizingly slow withdrawal from Vietnam and the ongoing debate about whether the war was correct or incorrect, moral or immoral, took a tremendous toll on college students. No one knew where the protests would lead. Although Richard Nixon had promised to end the war and troops were being withdrawn, the uncertainty of how long the war would last and how it would affect everyone's life cast a pall over the early part of the decade.

The years of the Nixon presidency (1969-1974) were times of tremendous turmoil. Whitworth students, with much of the rest of the country, continued to grapple with the implications of the assassinations of Martin Luther King, Jr. and Robert Kennedy in 1968. The struggle to overcome racism and the desire to avoid the mistakes of the past were complicated by Watergate and the question of what constitutes appropriate loyalty to one's country.

More than a few Whitworth students anguished over decisions about the length of their hair, the use of drugs, new forms of religious expression, and premarital sex. Young men spent long hours searching their souls, deciding whether to go to seminary. For many, the lure of a

draft deferment was a powerful inducement. The question of whether or not to enlist in one of the "safer" forms of military service such as the National Guard also presented a difficult choice. The initiation of the lottery system in the fall of 1969 brought the prospect of fighting in Vietnam even closer.

Whitworth men, like most college-age males of their generation, grappled with the moral dilemmas: stay and protest, accept the lottery, or move to Canada. The classroom often became a forum for such questions. Emotion and rancor often erupted; faculty and students divided into camps.

Facing Page - The Varsity Quartet (plus three) of 1973

Above - President Edward B. Lindaman (1970-1980): A visionary futurist from the space program

Speakers used Christianity to support contrary positions. There were no easy answers to any questions raised. For much of the decade, Whitworth administrators, students, and faculty would struggle to find appropriate expression of their political and ethical values while attempting to hold on to what was good about Whitworth's past.

Whitworth trustees and faculty sought a president who would be responsive to the complex forces at work in American society and higher education. Edward B. Lindaman, inaugurated in February 1970, articulated a vision of hope in the midst of turmoil and became known throughout the country for futurist thinking.

Lindaman came to the presidency from an executive position in the aerospace industry. He brought an outstanding record of lay leadership in the Presbyterian Church. A compelling speaker with great personal charisma, he attracted national attention to the college through his off-campus activities.

On campus, he assembled a team of new young administrators who brought some of the most recent theories in higher education to the Whitworth campus.

In many ways, Lindaman embraced the spirit of change and reform that had emerged in American society during the late 1960s. Most students and younger faculty believed he represented

Above - *Whitworth students march in downtown Spokane against the war in Vietnam (1970)*

Facing Page Bottom - *Challenging the establishment: Mark Cutshall tells his rabbit jokes at the Spring Easter Dinner in East Warren*

Left - *A Children's Theater was Whitworth's contribution to Spokane's Expo '74 World's Fair*

a progressive spirit that would make Whitworth a leader among Christian colleges in the 1970s. Without question, Lindaman's presence defused an element of on-campus student protest. He encouraged experimentation with curriculum and argued that education must be much more responsive to the rapidly changing forces in society. For some faculty, however, the new president represented too much change and not enough stability.

Even for Lindaman, however, the pace of student activism during the decade often proved difficult to guide and shape. Issues ranged from the war and civil rights to human sexuality and the environment. On April 22, 1970, Whitworth students participated in the National Ecology Teach-in, better known as Earth Day. Whitworth students spent the day cleaning the grounds from the Pirate's Cove to the baseball diamond.

Whitworth students' political attitudes began to change between the mid-'60s and early '70s. Historically very conservative, Whitworth students' reaction to the presidential candidacy of Senator Eugene McCarthy demonstrated their shift to greater liberalism. In 1968, while McCarthy mobilized college supporters across the country with his views against the war in Vietnam, at Whitworth he received little support. However, in 1972, again as an anti-war candidate, the Minnesota Democrat received a very favorable welcome from the Whitworth students when he spoke in Forum that May.

Racism discussions continued. Many students demanded greater commitment and resources for recruitment of minorities, specifically blacks. Students increased the pressure for more black professors, coaches, and Afro-American courses, more scholarship money, and financial aid. In 1974, a black theme dorm housed fourteen black students and six white students. The highlight of the year for the group was having national civil rights leader Ralph Abernathy to dinner. That same spring, Whitworth student Jacque Frazier was selected Miss Black Spokane.

By the end of the decade, however, Whitworth, like most small liberal arts institutions, had failed to achieve a significant population of minority students. The college did not have the resources to attract many black faculty members; consequently black students tended to gravitate to institutions that could.

Other concerns attracted student protest as well. A demonstration erupted over removing trees for lane expansion of Hawthorne Road. Pickets waving American flags temporarily halted the project, but eventually the road went through.

Whitworth and Gonzaga students organized protests when President Nixon came to open Spokane's Expo '74 World's Fair. Others put their energies into concern for the environment, which was the fair's theme. When Watergate became a national issue, many students called for Nixon's impeachment.

Protest was not Whitworth's only response to Expo '74, however. Reflecting a growing sense of community service, the college decided to stage a children's theatre at the fair. A 50-foot geodesic dome

Right - "Death of a
Salesman": Production
starred (l to r) Homer
Mason (Spokane Civic
Theater), Holly Sheehy,
Bruce Clizbe and
David Johnstone

Below Right - "The
Night Thoreau Spent
in Jail": Steven Hites
earned praise for his
role in this 1974 theatre
production

just north of the Washington State Pavilion on the south bank of the Spokane River housed the troupe of eight directed by Al Gunderson, chairman of the Whitworth Speech and Drama Department. The company wrote its own scripts and performed three fifty-minute shows a day. Though artistically acclaimed, the theatre only brought in enough to pay day-to-day expenses. None of the $26,000 invested by faculty, students, administrators, and other supporters could be repaid.

Professors Gunderson and Pat Stien continued to develop the tradition of great theater at the college. Building on the work of Loyd Waltz, the program in the '60s and '70s centered on a combination of Shakespearean drama and more contemporary offerings. In 1975, Stephen Hites, who played the lead in the production, "The Night Thoreau Spent in Jail," was selected to compete at the American College Theatre Festival in Eugene, Oregon. Several students went on to successful careers. David Johnstone, who studied acting at the Royal Academy for Dramatic Art, became a professional actor and taught a master class in mime for the famed Marcel Marceau. Doug MacIntyre, another gifted mime, performed his interpretations of symphonic music with the Boston Pops Orchestra and at Carnegie Hall. Toni Boggan became a television personality in Spokane, and Bruce (Clizbe) Talkington not only became a professional actor but also wrote for the Walt Disney Studios and earned an Emmy award for his "Winnie the Pooh" scripts. Rick Hornor, who starred in several student productions, came back to teach in the department beginning in 1985.

The Whitworth Choir's long-standing reputation for excellence continued in the 1960s and 1970s under the

direction of Milton Johnson. Professor Johnson spearheaded the annual "Messiah" performances, which grew into all-city affairs involving two hundred Whitworth singers and as many as eighty local school and church choirs. The event became a Spokane Christmas tradition, playing to full houses first in the Coliseum and later in the Opera House.

Johnson led the Whitworth Choir on yearly tours throughout the west coast and Hawaii. One year, the choir toured Europe, performing in Edinburgh, Coventry Cathedral, and Amsterdam. Through the years, the choir welcomed the pre-med and math major as well as the music major. The choir truly reflected a cross-section of the student body, and the campus community as a whole took pride in it.

By the 1970s, *The Whitworthian* had earned recognition as one of the leading college newspapers in the country. The paper's quality reflected the leadership of Al Gray, who was honored in 1979 as Distinguished Newspaper Advisor in the United States. *The Whitworthian* under his direction received ten first-class ratings

and sixteen all-American ratings from the Associated College Press. In 1975-76, the Western Washington chapter of the Society of Professional Journalists named *The Whitworthian* the best private college newspaper in the state. Professor Gray advised the paper for thirty-three years.

The changing social priorities of the late '60s and early '70s took a toll on several Whitworth traditions, most notably homecoming. By 1972, homecoming no longer included the traditional naming of a queen. Still interested in holding a banquet, dance, and football game, students sought to reflect an altruistic spirit in what they did. "Whitworth's Student Senate hopes to get the campus into the spirit of the game by changing the emphasis from Homecoming Royalty to student concern. The object is to involve everyone in a money-raising project to help support the Shriner's Hospital for Crippled Children," reported *The Whitworthian*, October 6, 1972. Football players visited children in the hospital. Car rallies, bake sales, and profits from ticket sales for the game with the University of Puget Sound all went to this worthy cause.

Above - Students organized enterprises such as the Co-op

Above Left - *Duncan Ferguson leading small group devotions: He served as chaplain, chair of the Religion department, V.P. for academic affairs and acting president for a year*

Above Right - *Academic Dean David Winter: One of "Captain Eddie's" cabinet members*

Lower Left - *"A One and a...": Choral Director Milton Johnson*

Lower Right - *English Professor Phil Eaton*

In response to students' interest in social issues, faculty worked at making the curriculum more responsive to the times. The 4-1-4 system, which had been approved in 1967 during President Koehler's term, was fully implemented in the 1968-69 school year. January Term, in which students took one course for the month, allowed both students and faculty to create new learning experiences.

Majors and student-designed areas of concentration became popular. These and other innovations developed in the late '60s were brought to fruition under the direction of David Winter, and Duncan Ferguson, who succeeded Winter as academic vice-president.

Also conceived and implemented in the late 1960s, the Core curriculum flowered in the 1970s. Under the leader-

ship of professors Clarence Simpson, Fenton Duvall, Leonard Oakland, and later Forrest Baird, the Core program provided students with a common intellectual experience. Core 150 focused on the Judeo-Christian tradition. Dr. Simpson's rendition of Moses' farewell address to the Israelites, in which he exhorted God's people to obey the Law and choose life over death, made an indelible imprint on many students' minds.

Core 250 took students from the philosophies of Plato and Aristotle to those of modern existentialists in order to give them an understanding of the essentials of Western thought and the roots of their own assumptions.

Students shared the common experience of studying late into the evening for a Core exam and years later alumni still recall their Core classes as pivotal moments in their intellectual life.

In the Biology department, Howard Stien, David Hicks, Jacqueline Fick, and Nicolin Gray mentored several Whitworth students including Keith Benson, Jim Maki, Dave Maloney, Drew Stevick, Debbie Engles, Jeff Hansen and Lisa Sardinia. These students went on to distinguished careers in medicine, research, and education.

By the 1970s, the English depart-

ment had earned a reputation as one of the most demanding as well as most stimulating on campus. In addition to Clarence Simpson and Lew Archer, Phil Eaton, Dean Ebner, Leonard Oakland, and Laura Bloxham all created exciting classroom experiences. The department attracted students who pursued a wide variety of careers. Graduates from the decade, including Mary Dewey and Laurie Lamon, went on to graduate school and later returned to Whitworth to teach. Russell Working, a student in the late '70s, received the Iowa Short Fiction award in 1986. The department also appealed to people who double-majored in English and the sciences: Linda Grund later studied epidemiology at Berkeley and Tim Evans did graduate work in medical research.

Professors Harry Dixon and George Weber led the Business and Economics department through the '70s. Professor Ernestine Evans retired in 1971 after thirty years of service to the college. During the decade, Ken Leonard helped develop the Center for Economic Education, which helped area public-school teachers acquire resources and new teaching techniques. Outstanding graduates from the decade included Bill Curry, who became president of Huntron Instruments in Seattle;

Above - Harry Dixon: Business and economics professor who was a popular personality on campus

Greg Hatch, president of Gross/Hatch Advertising in Spokane; and Bob Howell, who became a vice president for human resources with Christa Ministries.

Frank Houser in sociology and Norman Krebs in philosophy provided faculty leadership during the decade. F. Dale Bruner, Roger Mohrlang, and Duncan Ferguson joined the Religion Department. Professor Bruner's teaching of the Gospel of Mark became one of the most popular courses on campus.

The History and Political Studies department which included Homer Cunningham, Fenton Duvall, Garland "Gus" Haas, Dan Sanford and Jim Hunt turned out an extraordinary number of lawyers and graduate school students. Outstanding graduates from the decade included Colleen Redmond, who earned a doctorate in European history from Stanford University; Mark Valeri, currently teaching history at Lewis and Clark College, winner of the Burlington-Northern award for outstanding teaching; and Scott Rozelle, who earned his doctorate from Cornell and did postdoctoral research in Beijing.

Forum, a twice-weekly lecture and cultural series, began in the early '70s in response to student criticism of chapel. In 1969 students were still assigned seats for two chapels and one convocation per week. In 1970, administrators instituted an honor system of attendance, but this, as a *Whitworthian* editorial sarcastically said, "showed how many honorable people were on campus." Forum was initiated in 1971 and gave one quarter-credit based on at least 50 percent attendance. Designed to bring faculty, students, and administrators together to consider current issues, Forum became a major part of Whitworth's intellectual life. A sampling of the 1971 programs included a performance by the New Hope singers; a Homecoming musical; a film, "The Pleasure Seekers"; a lecture by Dr. Hippocrates, a columnist from the *Berkeley Barb*; lectures by Dr. Clarence Simpson and Dr. Dave Erb; and the choir performing selections from *Jesus Christ, Superstar*. While criticisms of the Forum program and the lack of student courtesy toward guest speakers would become a staple of life at Whitworth, the Forum concept endures much as originally envisioned. Alums fre-

Above and Left -
Fashion statement: Skirts got shorter, boots got longer and pantlegs got wider during the 1970s

Facing Page, Top -
Middle East adventure: Becky Nealy pictured on one of the overseas study tours that proliferated during the late 1960s and 70s

Facing Page, Bottom
Voyagers: Students paddled on the Arctic Barrens program in Northern Canada

quently speak of their memories of a moving speech or an artistic performance they witnessed in Forum and suggest that it was one of the best things about their education at Whitworth.

Students attended chapel on a voluntary basis, one day per week. Under first Duncan Ferguson and subsequently Ron White, Ron Frase, and Doug Dye, the chaplaincy program became a major part of the religious life of the campus. Dedicated in 1979, the Seeley Mudd Chapel provided a focal point for campus worship. Student leaders, with the assistance of college chaplains, made midweek worship an important part of the college's

life. Faculty often preached and the Whitworth Choir and the Chapel Singers frequently performed. The long tradition of the Whitworth community gathering regularly for reflection and worship continued.

In the 1970s, Whitworth began to find ways to move education outside the traditional classroom. In foreign studies programs, Whitworth students experienced European cultures as never before, and more study tours went to the Third World. In Central America, students witnessed deep social and political problems that challenged their middle-class values and their ability to apply a Christian ethic

Top Left - The Hippie: He grilled McMillan Hall freshmen to see if they had what it took to be a "Mac Man"

Bottom Left - The tent raising for 1971's "UNFAIR": Amusement rides, ecology displays and a concert by "The Association"

in a world with no easy answers. Living in homes and working side-by-side with Central Americans, Whitworth students often came back with a changed perspective. The venture of mind and spirit manifested itself in significant ways.

In the Arctic Barrens program, students spent six to eight weeks paddling and portaging through what was described as the "largest roadless area on the face of the planet." The Ragged Ridge Center for Environmental Education, a short-lived but ambitious program, envisioned Mount Spokane as an area where students could hike, camp, and study the environmental particulars of the high country.

Student concern for the environment and healthful living coalesced in one other program that received national attention—Nutrition 1985. Conceived by students in 1975, and guided by Professor Isla Rhodes, it focused both on eating more healthful foods and on integrating nutrition with economic, ecological, and political issues. Student organizers hoped that in ten years, all Whitworth students would be eating more responsibly. From a small gathering of a few students each noon, the program grew to occupy the downstairs dining room. Nutrition '85 helped raise the consciousness of many students. At various points in the decade, boycotts were staged against lettuce, bananas, and coffee; on at least one occasion the amount of food thrown away by students was put on display.

The concept of Student Development was one of the decade's major innovations. College administrators revamped life in the residence halls and altered the curriculum to reflect their conviction that Whitworth's most important goal was to prepare students for all of life. As students became more conscious of their own developmental process, life-style choices and ethical issues became hot topics in the dorm and the classroom. Vice President for Student Development David Erb and his staff took student input seriously and encouraged students to take responsibility for their actions.

Students asked for greater variety and choices in many areas. College offi-

cials responded by providing a number of different living environments. Theme and coeducational dorms were innovations of the early '70s. Calvin Hall housed artists. The Co-op Dorm held ten men and ten women who took responsibility for their own cooking and custodial work. The Interpersonal Skills Dorm worked together with the Human Identity Dorm to engage small groups in "finding the real meaning of being a man or woman." Twenty men and twenty women occupied the study dorms and two new coed traditional dorms housed twenty residents each.

The Village dorms, completed in 1975, received names from exotic languages: Akili, Tiki, Shalom, Keola, Charis, and Hobjob. In Charis, senior men and women sought to ease the transition to the working world after graduation. Sunday seminars addressed how to shop for insurance, how to finance a home and what records to keep for income tax purposes. The Shalom theme was community service. "Alternative Lifestyles" was the theme in Hobjob; discussions, research and independent studies focused on liv-

Above - Several long-time faculty retired: (l to r) Ruby Heritage (music), Russell Larson (art), Jasper Johnson (education), John Carlson (mathematics), Evelyn Smith (religion), Joan Larson (art), William Wilson (physics), Roland Wurster (English), Mae Whitten (English), Mary Elizabeth Waltz (music), Nicolin Gray (biology), Lillian Whitehouse (dean of women), Alfred Gray (journalism), Leonard Martin (music), Oscar Dismang (business), Homer Cunningham (history), Mrs. Dismang, R. Fenton Duvall (history) and Rhea French (library) - photo courtesy of Al Gray

ing in the country rather than in the suburbs. The Creative Writing dorm housed budding authors, and in the Twentieth Century history dorm, students invited young professors such as Dr. Jim Hunt to lead their discussions on historical topics.

For all the effort to create new living environments, some of the old persisted at McMillan Hall. Made up largely of former Westminster residents, the McMillan dorm quickly developed "new" traditions. Initiation turned into a major event. The extended ritual involved reciting dorm poems and singing dorm songs, doing hundreds of push-ups, performing gorilla stomps, and sitting in buckets of ice. For several years a figure known only as "the Hippie," attired in a spiked helmet and leather jacket, appeared during initiation week to see whether the proper McMillan spirit had been developed in each new "Mac Man." During these rites of passage, conducted around Labor Day weekend, the new freshmen were required to kneel in front of Ballard Hall and "sing 'White Christmas' until it snows." When it failed to snow, Mac upperclassmen would exhort the freshmen even more vehemently. Eventually, Ballard women would take pity and throw down Kleenex "snow" from third floor windows and save the initiates from further disgrace.

In the late 1970s, Community Building Day emerged in place of some aspects of freshmen orientation. Organ-

ized by the Student Development office, the morning was designed to develop campus unity and the afternoon was intended for dorm celebrations. A pancake breakfast began the day and outgoing dorm residents, dressed in slippers and robes, entertained eaters with songs and cheers. After breakfast came crash courses in folk and square dancing, human pyramids, a game combining soccer and slaughter ball, and jousting tournaments with students as both horses and knights. In many respects it was a throwback to the early Whitworth days when the Freshman and Sophomore classes roughhoused and played tug-of-war.

Students experimented with other forms of entertainment and attempted, if not to establish new traditions, at least to give them a new twist. The most ambitious effort was the UNFAIR in April, 1971. Described as a three-day extravaganza, the UNFAIR stressed community involvement, learning, and fun.

The highlight was a concert in the Pine Bowl by the popular singing group, The Association. Organizers optimistically expected that 30-35,000 would attend the event. Students leased seventeen amusement rides and set up fifteen game booths in the lot behind Warren Hall. Student art and local commercial exhibits along with previews of the EXPO '74 river beautification plans filled the Loop. A tent held a dozen scientific and ecological displays, and movies ran continuously in Cowles

Above - Studying in the Loop: These students take advantage of a sunny spring afternoon

Auditorium.

A slightly less spectacular but longer-lasting project was the effort to revive the campus radio station last heard in the 1950s. Meetings began in 1971, but it was 1975 before the efforts of Jon Flora and several other students achieved serious momentum. Finally, in September 1977, with help from journalism professor Al Gray and political science professor Gus Haas, radio station KWRS went on the air. It has been broadcasting ever since.

In sports, the decade began on a high note when former Washington State University pass-catching great, Hugh Campbell, agreed to be head football coach. After an all-pro career in the Canadian Football League, Campbell was attracted to Whitworth College largely for the same reasons others have come. "I wanted to coach at a smaller college where the proper emphasis was placed on athletics," said the ex-Cougar. He took over a team that had won but one game in each of the previous two seasons. From 1972 to 1976, his record was 30 wins and 16 losses. In 1975 Campbell led the Pirates into a tie for the Northwest Conference title. In 1975 and '76, wide receiver Doug Long achieved All-American honors. But in 1977, the Edmonton Eskimos of the CFL lured Campbell away to be their coach.

Many strong tennis teams in the '70s played under Coach Ross Cutter. Tennis players over the decades recall with great affection Coach Cutter's selection of outstanding restaurants in out-of-the-way locales. The ceremonial opening of the first tennis balls became a Whitworth tradition under Coach Cutter, who was named to the NAIA Tennis Coaches' Hall of Fame in 1986. Whitworth won the conference track championship in 1972 under Bruce Grambo. While basketball teams did not have extraordinary success, Coach Cal Riemke was highly regarded as an outstanding influence on young men's lives.

Under Coach Jean Anderson, the women's basketball team had several very successful years. In 1977 and 1978, they won the conference championship, with top athletes such as Paula Sporcic, Kivonne Tucker, and Meredith Jung. The women's volleyball team, under Peggy Warner, won the conference championship as well, in 1977. In the following year, the women's volleyball team played in the AIAW national tournament in Orlando. Under coach Joanne Atwell-Scrivner, in 1979, the

Above - Hugh Campbell: Pirate football coach who went on to lead professional teams in Edmonton and Houston

coach Terry Kelly. The 1979 team won the conference championship and competed in the nationals in Tallahassee, Florida.

Intramurals, as always, were popular. One fall count listed 1100 students in bowling, cross country, football, golf, one-pitch, soccer, and tennis.

Many faculty who were to make a substantial impact on students over the next decade came during the 1970s: Jean Anderson, Deane Arganbright, Laura Bloxham, Dale Bruner, Richard Evans, Duncan Ferguson, Ron Frase, Jim Hunt, Bob Lacerte, Don Liebert, Roger Mohrlang, Tammy Reid, Dan Sanford, Gordon Wilson and Michael Young all arrived during this time. This new generation succeeded several long-time faculty members who retired around the turn of the decade, including Al Quall, Homer Cunningham, Clarence Simpson, Ernestine Evans, Roland Wurster, Flaval Pearson, Evelyn Smith, Al Gray, and Nicolin Gray.

For much of the decade financial problems plagued the college. Deficits were not uncommon and this placed a particular strain on administration and faculty. Tuition had to be raised repeatedly and inflation took a significant toll on purchasing power. Students demanded

volleyball team competed in the national tournament in Los Angeles. In 1980, Whitworth hosted the national women's volleyball tournament and finished sixth. Several women's cross-country teams were very strong in the late '70s under

information regarding finances and fiscal decisions.

In 1978, President Lindaman and Provost Duncan Ferguson commissioned a twelve member Redesign Commission to revise the curriculum, strengthen majors, and make Whitworth more attractive to students. There was fear in the late '70s that the decline of available 18- to 24-year-olds would make it difficult to maintain enrollment at the 1200 level. Costs rose at ten percent a year and few people expressed optimism about the ability of the college to maintain the status quo. Faculty and administration often disagreed in the late '70s regarding the strategies for directing the college.

Eventually this conflict dampened even the enthusiasm of the irrepressible Lindaman. In the spring of 1979, he announced his resignation, effective February 1980. Despite the financial difficulties and general anxiety of the decade, Lindaman's vision for service and responsiveness to the needs of the world remained etched on the minds of the college community. The Board of Trustees honored him with the title of President Emeritus and Futurist in Residence. Tragically, however, President Lindaman died in 1982, after contracting viral encephalitis during a trip to China. All of Whitworth mourned his untimely passing. His spirit would be forever associated with the college in the 1970s.

Facing Page, Top - *Jim Larson coached the men's basketball squad, whose opponents faced verbal harassment from the football team in the "dog pound" behind the basket*

Above *- Kivonne Tucker is on the ball: Jean Anderson coached successful women's basketball teams*

Left *- Call her Spike: The Women's volleyball team went to the national tournament*

CHAPTER X - THE 1980s

A WORLD OF DIFFERENCE

Across the nation, the college generation of the 1980s turned in a more conservative direction compared to its predecessors. The ferment of the '60s and '70s had sapped the nation's energy for more social change. And economic problems that arose in the late '70s and early '80s caused many students and their parents to believe that a good job ought be their primary concern. Nationwide, business majors increased while interest in sociology, history, and philosophy declined.

Whitworth faculty members who had taught at the college during the '60s and '70s generally found the students more conservative than they were themselves. Business and accounting majors increased dramatically at Whitworth. The national resurgence of religious fundamentalism influenced life at the college. And in both 1980 and 1984, Whitworth students favored Ronald Reagan over Jimmy Carter and Walter Mondale by large majorities. George Bush bested Michael Dukakis in a campus election as well as in the nation in 1988.

The selection of Robert Mounce as Whitworth president in 1980 reflected this shift toward conservatism in the country as a whole. Dr. Mounce came to Whitworth from Western Kentucky University in Bowling Green, where he had served as dean for the previous eight years. Author of eight books, mostly biblical commentaries, Dr. Mounce was asked by trustees to move the college in a more evangelical direction.

Several seniors interviewed in *The Whitworthian* in 1984 felt the college was

Facing Page - Ballet thrived during the decade under Rita Rogers

Below - President Robert H. Mounce (1981-1987): A biblical scholar who emphasized Christian values at Whitworth

Top - Open door?: Director of minority affairs Rose Howell was in charge during an apartheid simulation that gave white students a taste of life as an oppressed majority

Bottom - Symbolic protest: Students remembered the victims of apartheid and called for Whitworth to divest from companies that do business in South Africa during Apartheid Awareness Week

becoming more conservative, although they focused primarily on the inability of their fellow students to raise serious questions in class. Polls of student attitudes during the period revealed that Whitworth students were neither overly conservative nor liberal. While a substantial majority believed homosexuality to be morally wrong, opinion was divided evenly on abortion and capital punishment.

Nevertheless, in the midst of forces leading in a more conservative direction, significant numbers of students were moved by issues of international human rights. In spring, 1987, Whitworth students staged Apartheid Simulation Day. Carrying passbooks, and having to enter doors at the backs of buildings, students attempted to empathize with the plight of blacks in South Africa. Several student leaders met with President Mounce, asking him and the Board of Trustees to review the college investment portfolio and to withdraw monies from companies doing business in South Africa. The board did review investments and attempted to reassure those concerned that Whitworth funds were not helping to support apartheid.

During the spring of 1988, Michael LeRoy and other students organized a Human Rights Awareness Week. Attempting to bring attention to the problems of living in a militarist state, students created a simulated coup d'etat. Dressed in military garb, student Marty Miller took control of the campus. Students were arrested and detained without trial. Speakers from Amnesty International came to campus, and students listened to a debate on the death penalty. When political activist and well-known actor Ed Asner spoke on campus against U.S. foreign policy in Central America, several Spokane community residents picketed outside the campus gate in protest.

Study tours to Central America, under professors Ron Frase, Don Liebert, Ed Miller, Jim Hunt, Ross Cutter, and Joanne Atwell-Scrivner had profound influence on the lives of many students in the '80s. Encouraged to work for peace and justice issues, several students came

Left - *Springfest '88: Students stacked Oreo cookies to raise money for charity*

Below - *Helping Habitat for Humanity: President Arthur J. De Jong at building site with student volunteers (l-r) Tracy (T.J.) Sims, Jim Bennett, Juli Duffus, Michael Barram and Nancy Gronhovd*

back to campus and worked for organizations such as Amnesty International.

Students also invested energy in domestic social issues. In 1987, they staged Springfest in Spokane's Riverfront Park and raised $3000 for the Ronald McDonald House, a locally-funded inn for the families of children with terminal illnesses. That fall, Whitworth student Kurt Liebert organized the "Colossal Moronathon," a parody of an ironman triathlon that had the inspired lunacy of a Monty Python sketch. Students competed in a slow run, silly walk, and one-lap swim to raise money for the Habitat for Humanity Program in Pancasan, Nicaragua, and for the local Spokane Habitat group. Whitworth students rallied to the Habitat for Humanity goal, which was to build no-profit/no-interest homes for America's working poor. Whitworth, led by student Michael Barram, became the fifth college in the country to organize its own chapter of Habitat for Humanity. For his efforts, Barram was privileged to meet with former president Jimmy Carter, one of Habitat's leading supporters. Benefit events and fundraising for this and other causes were frequent campus activities during the last half of the decade.

One of the more unusual efforts at fundraising came over the Thanksgiving break in 1989. Mason Marsh and

Thomas Lynch organized the "Race and Mase in Your Face Marathon Telethon Phenomenon." The enterprising pair stayed on the air at KWRS (Whitworth's radio station) for 82 consecutive hours and raised over $850 for the Union Gospel Mission.

Tony Campolo, founder and president of the Evangelical Association for the Promotion of Education, spoke at Whit-

Top - *Worship service in Seeley Mudd Chapel*

Bottom - *Chaplain Ron Frase*

ministries in Northern Ireland and Mexico. Faculty contributions to the auction ranged from the shaving of Professor Lew Archer's beard to songs of the '60s performed by the History and Political Studies department's version of Peter, Paul and Mary (professors Arlin Migliazzo, Dale Soden, and Kathy Lee). English Professor Vic Bobb offered to write a short story, with two Whitworth students as the main characters, guaranteed to include "guilt, love, passion, and sentimentality."

In the fall of 1989, Whitworth students participated in a week-long "Racial Awareness Project." Featuring several off-campus speakers, African dance and musical performances, articles in *The Whitworthian*, and faculty-student workshops, the project focused campus attention on the continued problem of racism in American society as well as the ongoing struggle for Whitworth to attract significant numbers of racial and ethnic minorities.

The hottest on-campus issue of the decade was 24-hour visitation in the dormitories. By mid-decade, among several administrators, faculty members and trustees as well as a significant number of students, there was growing discomfort with the 24-hour visitation privilege in the residence halls. After an exchange of proposals and counter-proposals in 1987, it appeared that visitation would be restricted. Students staged a sit-down demonstration in support of the existing pol-

worth several times during the decade and challenged Whitworth students to come and work with him in the slums of Philadelphia. Students responded by organizing an auction that raised more than $2,500 for Diakonia, Whitworth's summer mission program for students. The money helped pay expenses and transportation for student volunteers to New York and to Mother Teresa's Missionaries of Charity, to Tony Campolo's program for underprivileged children, and other

icy. Just under 500 students signed petitions demanding the right to set visiting hours, and threatening to leave Whitworth if their demands were denied. When the dust settled, 24-hour visitation remained, along with a process called Community Values Implementation, instituted by the Office of Student Life. This system allowed each dormitory to establish certain rules and penalties by a vote of the participants.

The Office of Student Life, under Dean Julia Anderton, also sponsored week-long discussions and seminars on issues such as alcohol and human sexuality. Greg Hamann, associate dean of students, and Rhonda Koele, director of the Health Center, coordinated guest experts, counselors, and professors who made presentations and led small-group discussions to encourage decision-making. Professors Kyle and Kathy Storm, among others, led students through serious discussions regarding the dynamics of sexuality and human relationships. The coordinators of the 1987 Human Sexuality Week articulated four goals: 1) That Whitworth be established as a safe place for honesty and openness about sexuality. 2) That we acknowledge our sexuality as a gift from God, and as a part of our being

in the image of God. 3) That we understand the ways in which our bodies, emotions, values, and faith can work in forming a base for responsible decision-making. 4) That we have adequate knowledge of the issues and resources related to our sexuality.

Residence halls began to seek their own individual images. McMillan, with its long tradition as a male dorm, led the way with Mac Hall in Concert, a major entertainment event each spring. Begun in 1974, Mac Hall in Concert featured

Top - *Dorm life in Arend Hall: (l to r) Kristen Johnson, Kim Gray and Daphne Howe*

Bottom - *History professor Jim Hunt and students in an informal setting*

Above Left - Mac
Attack: A water
balloon fight in front
of McMillan Hall

Above Right -
Psychology professor
Pat MacDonald

home-grown talent, comedy, dancing, and music in a format not totally unlike the minstrel shows of Whitworth's Tacoma years. Though auditions were required, occasionally the bizarre slipped through — such as a goldfish-in-a-blender act. But for the most part, the event featured quality acts from students and faculty. It was so popular that in 1985, for example, 38 acts competed for 15 available slots in the show.

Every year the Mac men sought some way to wreak their own special havoc. In 1988, Mac men set 1,000 crickets free in Stewart. But other dorms contributed their own unique flavor to campus life. One year, a "Men of Stewart" pinup calendar was a big success. And when a decision came to convert the hall to coed, Stewart men rallied for the status quo with a "Save the Urinals" campaign.

A slightly more organized activity that emerged on campus in the '80s was tennis ball golf. Played with a seven-iron and a tennis ball, the game ranged

over much of the campus. Players hacked their way from "hole" to "hole," undoing the good efforts of the grounds crew. The annual Tom Taylor tournament culminated with the ceremonial awarding of the "Green Jacket" (a 7-UP Bottling Company sportcoat) to the champion.

After falling on hard times in the '70s, Homecoming regained its place among Whitworth traditions. Again students built floats for the parade and held class competitions: a rootbeer chug, Volkswagen stuff, pie-eating contest, iron man competition and talent shows. In 1985, a pep rally in the Aquatic Center included a slide show, food, "dunk the execs" competition, cheers, and speeches. A Homecoming coronation and dance at Cavanaugh's Inn at the Park, in downtown Spokane, climaxed the weekend.

Students continued to enjoy moments when the faculty made fun of themselves. The 1989 version of McEachran Hall in concert found President De Jong adorned by the ever-popular Mickey Mouse ears. Emceed by Kyle Storm and professor Gordon Jackson, the popular event featured Darrell and Judy Guder on the piano, Ed Olson and Ross Cutter in their timeless basketball sketch, football coach Shorty Bennett leading a rock and roll band, and Mike Westenskow demonstrating the art of removing a light bulb. Julie Anderton and Don Liebert teamed in a skit as did Rick Hornor and Pat Stien. Perhaps the show stoppers of the evening, however, were Mrs. Miller and the Miller-lites (Janet Yoder, Tammy Reid, Kathy Lee, Kathy Storm, Linda Hunt, Doris Liebert, and Sue Jackson), lip-syn-

ching and dancing to several songs. The concert ended on a slightly higher note when Whitworth students heard the tremendous vocal talents of soprano Ann Fennessy.

Renewed interest in ASWC (Associated Students of Whitworth College) began in the middle of the decade. J. B. Meade won two successive terms as student body president and participation increased. Many hours went into drafting new forms of governance and more students ran for office and voted.

Whitworth's reputation for producing outstanding artistic performances grew throughout the decade. Professor Richard Evans provided overall Fine Arts leadership. Under Rita Rogers, the ballet program at the college grew remarkably in numbers, reputation, and scope. Starting with almost no funding, Ms. Rogers made a considerable impact not only on her students but on ballet in Spokane. The students she took to New York City for January Term were praised by the professionals, and the annual dance performances became a highlight of the cultural

year. Most noteworthy were the full ballets, *Copelia* and *Romeo and Juliet*.

Randi Von Ellefson came in 1984, and soon gained international recognition for his direction of the Whitworth Choir. The Christmas concerts under Ellefson became major productions, and the spring tours proved to be spiritual and artistic successes, as well as very effective recruiting tools. The choir continued to generate enormous pride through-

Top - *Whitworth's choir gained international recognition under director Randi Von Ellefson*

Bottom - *Aloha!: Hawaiian students entertained at their annual Luau*

Above - "People Will Say We're in Love": Doug Wunsch and Ruthanne LeLaCheur sang in a 1982 production of "Oklahoma"

Bottom - World class: Professor Leonard Oakland led this study tour to France in 1986

out the campus community.

In 1982, Margaret Ott retired after teaching piano for twenty-two years at the college. Her influence on and inspiration to students over the near quarter century became almost legend. One of her most successful students was Greg Slag. After graduating in 1983, Slag studied at the Juilliard School, where he received the coveted William Petschek Piano Debut Award in 1988. A prizewinner in several international competitions, Greg has played to critical acclaim in Lincoln Center.

Professor Pauline Haas retired from the Art Department in 1985 after teaching eleven years at the college. Professor Haas helped develop the painting talents of countless students during her years at the college.

The jazz music program earned regional recognition under the direction of Dan Keberle, who came to Whitworth in 1988. In its first major competition the jazz choir, under Shawn Wright, took first place in the College Vocal Division of the Lionel Hampton Jazz Festival at the University of Idaho. Professor Keberle directed the Jazz Ensemble to a second-place award in the Instrumental Division at the same festival in 1989.

Under professors Pat Stien and Rick Hornor, Whitworth students performed in acclaimed musical and dramatic productions such as "Oklahoma," "Music Man," "Luther," and Arthur Miller's "The Crucible." One of the more popular productions was "Damn Yankees," in 1987. Starring Tom Tavener, Jim Bennett, Jennifer Kallenberg , John Sowers, and Elizabeth Zirkle among a host of others, the production received excellent reviews.

Academic Vice Presidents Richard Ferrin and Darrell Guder wielded

Left - *Academics of the 80s: (l to r) Howard Stien (biology), Dean Darrell Guder, Gordon Jackson (communications) and Associate Dean Tammy Reid*

Below Left - *Music Professor Margaret Ott retired in 1982 after teaching piano at Whitworth for twenty-two years*

Below Right - *Uneasy perch: Jim Bennett rides on James Holsworth (l) and Ken Urie in the 1986 theater production of "Damn Yankees"*

significant influence over the direction of the college. Dr. Guder, along with Dan Sanford, professor of history/political studies, helped to develop an increased emphasis on overseas programs and international students. Sanford led the way in developing affiliations with colleges and universities in the Far East. Dean Guder instituted a Berlin Study tour to help complement the existing Central America, France, and British Isles tours. Janet Yoder developed an English Language Program for international students who came to Whitworth as well as a major summer program for Asian students.

In 1989, faculty approved the development of the Master's Degree in Cross-Cultural Studies, Whitworth's contribution to the Spokane Intercollegiate Research and Technical Institute (S.I.R.T.I.), a unique consortium of Washington State University, Eastern Washington University, the Community Colleges of Spokane and Gonzaga University. By the end of the decade Whitworth had received funding to help twenty faculty become bi-lingual in order to facilitate cross-cultural perspective in the classroom.

Other funding materialized late in the decade, largely with the assistance of Charles Wait, the academic grant writer.

Right - High tech:
Computers entered
more classrooms,
thanks to a major grant
landed by (l to r)
director of academic
computing Ken Pecka,
mathematics professor
Howard Gage and di-
rector of computer edu-
cation Randy Michaelis

Below - English
professor Laura
Bloxham earned
Washington state
"Professor of the Year"
honors in 1988 from
C.A.S.E. (Council for
Advancement and Sup-
port of Education)

Linda Hunt directed a program in writing across the curriculum which assisted professors in all disciplines with their instruction of the writing process.

Whitworth's greatest influence, however, seemed to be in the number of graduates earning certification in teaching. Throughout the region, but particularly in eastern Washington, Whitworth graduates received acclaim for their teaching expertise. Under Shirley Richner,

placement of Whitworth graduates was extraordinarily high. At the graduate level, Betty Malmstad directed a very successful program, with as many as 500 students pursuing advanced degrees at the college. Margo Long developed a Gifted and Talented program that received regional recognition.

Academic computing emerged during the decade as a major feature of campus life for both faculty and students. By the 1980s the level of computing far exceeded the days in the early '70s when Bob McCroskey and Hugh Johnston worked with a key-punch. During the first few years, the punched cards were sent by Greyhound bus to Washington State University, processed and then returned by bus. By 1982, however, the faculty approved a computer science major. Howard Gage successfully wrote a grant proposal in 1984 to establish a computer education program; in 1988, Professors Gage and Randy Michaelis, along with Ken Pecka and Bob McCroskey, persuaded the Murdock Foundation to provide $652,000 for academic computing. By the end of the decade, it was almost as common for students to bring their personal computers with them as it had been for students to bring their stereos in the 1960s.

In addition to improvements in

computing, the chemistry department benefitted from grants received from the Burlington Northern Foundation, the Perkin-Elmer Corporation, and the National Science Foundation, as well as several large gifts from alums to upgrade equipment.

The desire to understand the role of technology from an interdisciplinary perspective, combined with the efforts of several alums and friends of the college to perpetuate the legacy of Ed Lindaman, led to the establishment of an endowed chair, the Lindaman Chair of Communications, Technology, and Change. The first occupant, Robert Wauzzinski came in 1986 and combined research, teaching, and community speaking.

During this decade, *U.S. News & World Report* and *New York Times Books* recognized Whitworth as one of the top liberal arts schools in the West. In 1988, Laura Bloxham, professor of English, was selected as Washington State's "Professor of the Year" by the Council for the Advancement and Support of Education, an international organization of colleges and universities. Dr. Bloxham began teaching in 1975 and developed an outstanding reputation, not only among traditional undergraduate students but also community members who took her annual literature seminars. In addition, professors John Yoder, Dan Sanford and Arlin Migliazzo in history/political studies and Deane Arganbright in mathematics were awarded Fulbright fellowships to teach in Liberia, Korea, and New Guinea.

The Burlington Northern Foundation provided funds to help honor outstanding teaching. Award winners during the decade included: Duncan Ferguson, Pierrette Gustafson, Randi Ellefson, Lois Kieffaber, Pat Stien, Kathy Storm, Roger Mohrlang, Martha Nelson, Shirley Richner, and Raja Tanas.

The long-awaited Aquatic Center opened in March, 1985. Only two years after the pool opened, Whitworth hosted the 1987 NAIA National Swimming and Diving Championships. A year later, officials selected Whitworth to be the village for the U.S. Olympic Cycling Trials in preparation for the Olympic games in Seoul, South Korea. Also in the late '80s, a $7 million bond issue funded renovation of the campus residence halls, paving,

landscaping and classroom upgrading.

The athletic successes of the '80s were measured largely in individual accomplishments. Dave Pomante and Randy Burkhart were named All-American football players in 1980 and '83 respectively. In football, Wayne Ralph set the NAIA single-season pass reception record in 1985 and 1986, and broke NAIA records for average catches per game and single-season yardage. During his career, Ralph broke virtually all of Whitworth's pass-receiving records and was awarded All-American honors in 1985 and '86. In 1988, running back Mark Linden became the first Pirate player in twenty-five years to rush for more than 1,000 yards in a season; in the following year, Linden broke Charlie Reed's single-game rushing record, which had stood since 1962, by rushing for 255 yards.

Coach Jim Larson led several basketball teams to successful seasons, including 1981-82, when the Pirates went

Above - Religion professor Dale Bruner listens to a student's opinion

Above - On the right track: Coach Scott McQuilkin's 1987 team won district and came within one out of going to the NAIA World Series; seniors (l to r) Ian Cameron, Troy Anderson, Brian Cook, Brian Parisotto, Ryan Clements, Scott Barkley, Vern Hare, Scott Carolan and Jeff Bare

Right- In the swim: New Aquatic Center was dedicated in 1985

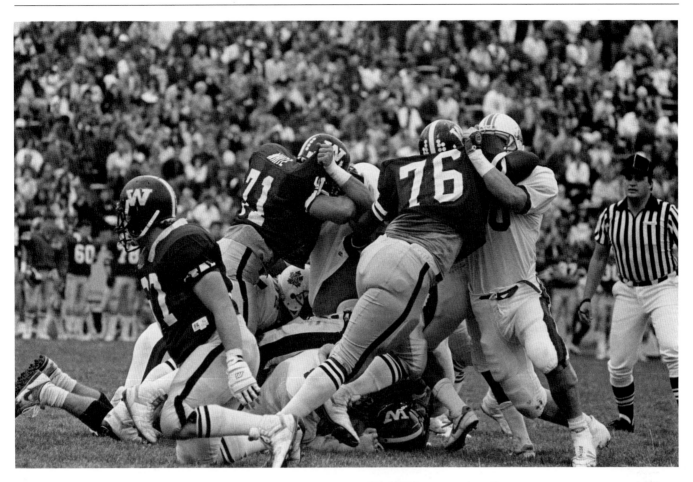

18-10 and won the conference championship, but lost in the playoffs for a trip to the NAIA tournament in Kansas City. The following year they repeated as champions of the Northwest Conference with a 20-7 record, led by a tenacious defense that ranked second nationally, allowing just 57.8 points per game. Again, however, they lost in the playoffs and failed to make the national tournament. In 1985, Warren Friedrichs began as head basketball coach and in 1989 led the Bucs again to the district playoffs.

The Pirate baseball team emerged as the most consistently successful during the decade. Led by Scott McQuilkin, Coach of the Year in 1987 and 1989, the Buc baseball team won three district championships, in 1984, '87, and '89. In cross-country, Chris Paul competed at the nationals in 1985. The following year, Kelli Burch earned All-American honors in cross-country. Coached by Andy Sonneland, Evan Coates and Melanie Kosin earned All-American honors at the NAIA cross-country championships in 1989. In 1981, Doug Larson established a NAIA record in the decathlon which remained unbroken at the end of the decade. In 1987 and '88, under Track and Field Coach Arnie Tyler, Whitworth produced a na-

Above - *A game of inches: Coaches Bruce Grambo and Whitworth alum Blaine "Shorty" Bennett directed Pirate football during the 1980s*

Left - *Tommy Stewart: The 1984 national champion in the long jump, he led a steady stream of track and field All-Americans coached by Arnie Tyler*

tionally ranked hammer squad led by Tim Jacobson. His wife Kari set Whitworth records for the indoor 55-meter hurdles and 500-meter event as well as outdoor records in several events. By the time Tyler retired in 1989, he had coached twenty-three All-Americans including Barb Lashinski-Johnson, the first three-time All-American in Whitworth history, who won the competition in the javelin in the 1987 NAIA championships and finished second in 1989. The women's tennis program gained success under Jo Wagstaff, 1987's Coach of the Year.

The men's soccer team won the league championship in 1988 and Einar Thorarinsson earned Coach of the Year honors as well. In 1989, the soccer team accomplished a major upset when it defeated the University of Washington, a team ranked 18th in the nation at the NCAA division one level. The Pirates were the first team in five years to defeat the Huskies on their home field. John Gould received All-American honors. Women's volleyball teams won several conference championships, and twelve swimmers went to national championships in 1987. Swim Coach Tom Dodd was also Coach of the Year in 1989.

By the 1980s, commencement traditions had fully developed. They included Senior Honors Forum, in which departments lauded students' outstanding achievements and students named their Most Influential Professor of the Year. Those honored professors included Harry Dixon, Leonard Oakland, Michael DeGolyer, and Forrest Baird. On the Saturday before commencement, Professor Emeritus Homer Cunningham coordinated the Homer Alder Memorial Golf Tournament at Wandermere. Picnic in the Loop and Concert in the Park by the Wind Ensemble became traditional as did the Senior Reflections talent show and dessert on Saturday night. On Saturday or Sunday morning, departments hosted brunches or held receptions for seniors. One of the most moving traditions came at the end of baccalaureate service when Professor Leonard Oakland led the audience in singing "Amazing Grace," to which he added his own special Whitworth verses. For most of the decade, commencement took place at the Opera House in downtown Spokane, at which time the President's Cups, Servant Leader awards, and honorary degrees were awarded.

In 1987, Dr. Mounce announced that he would retire prior to the beginning of fall classes. That fall, the search committee selected Arthur De Jong, then president of Muskingum College in New Concord, Ohio, to be Whitworth's 16th president. The new president assumed his position on February 1, 1988, and began immediately preparing for the fundraising associated with the college centennial in 1990. Known for his administrative success at Muskingum, De Jong set the tone for his administration by challenging the faculty to take seriously the mix of Christianity and liberal arts.

De Jong institutionalized long-range planning as the college attempted to preserve the strengths of its past and look forward with clearer purpose and mission. Professor Kathryn Lee chaired the committee which authored the long-range report. Approved overwhelmingly by both faculty and trustees, the document will serve as the blueprint for Whitworth's next five years. Under alums Chuch Boppell and Jon Flora, the largest fundraising campaign in the history of the college was launched in the fall of 1989 amid hot air balloons and a campus-wide picnic. A major addition to the library, a new student union building, and improvements to the athletic facilities highlighted the goals of the capital campaign.

After a stabilizing decade, Whitworth renewed its moorings in the Reformed tradition and more confidently asserted that its niche was as a Christian liberal arts institution with high academic standards. Its vision focused on the importance of cross-cultural understanding and service to humankind.

The 1989-90 school year opened a year of celebration for Whitworth's centennial. Centering on the theme "Making a World of Difference," Dr. De Jong focused the attention of the entire Whit-

Facing Page, Top - To the hoop: Guard Steve Mihas drives for another Pirate basket.

Facing Page, Bottom Women's basketball: Jennifer Crowe shoots over Simon Fraser as Tara Flugel and Tracy Brooks get position.

Left - Philosophy Professor Forrest Baird

Below - Centennial Celebration: Balloons are launched from the centennial plaza to kickoff the fifteen-million dollar capital campaign

worth community on the achievements of the past and present, emphasizing the consistency of the vision of "the education of heart and mind" that had directed Whitworth's first century. Whitworth's centennial celebration featured artistic events, public lectures, and campus-wide activities that helped not only Whitworth, but the city of Spokane as well, to commemorate the significance of 100 years of existence. George Whitworth would have enjoyed the party.

EPILOGUE

Shortly after I arrived at Whitworth in 1985, a colleague, who had taught at the college for nearly twenty years, shared with me his impressions. He expressed great satisfaction at the number of students who had found this a good place to ask tough questions. In the midst of difficult times over the last two decades, he said, Whitworth had provided students with a supportive Christian environment and challenging academic standards. And he spoke almost glowingly of the number of students who had developed a world view oriented toward serving humankind.

Last spring, for the first time, I watched the graduation of students I had known since they were freshmen. As they walked across the stage, I remembered that conversation, and I felt the same sense of pride. So many of my students had inspired me: Jeff Mullaney, who had struggled to find meaning and purpose in the poverty and anguish he witnessed while working in Haiti; Joel Fielder, a Spokane fireman, who spent nearly seven years working his way through evening college to complete his degree in accounting. Every one of my colleagues has been enriched by the lives of hundreds of students as they have passed through this college.

I have also come to be moved and inspired by my colleagues. The effort made to create an exciting classroom experience, the empathy demonstrated for students of very diverse backgrounds, and the energy expended to improve the quality of this institution have made a deep impression on me in four short years.

At the risk of sounding trite, I am convinced that the guiding vision of educating both heart and mind, established by George Whitworth and that first generation, continues to serve the college well. The persistence of hundreds of individuals—led by faith in Christ's redemption, in believing that Christian higher education has a critical role to play in not only the lives of individual students but for society as well — has helped create a dynamic institution.

Within American higher education in the twentieth century, a majority of colleges and universities once affiliated with a religious denomination have significantly altered that relationship. Either the ties have been severed completely or the connection with the church has withered into mere formality. Whitworth's history has been different. Whitworth is among a select few colleges that have remained remarkably true to the vision of its founding generation.

At times Whitworth faculty, administration, and students have been more successful than at others in implementing that vision. At certain moments, external forces in American culture as well as financial difficulties have made the fulfillment of academic excellence in a Christian context especially difficult. Certainly the problems in finding a permanent campus, the closing of the college during the First World War, and the fire that destroyed Ballard Hall all made the fulfillment of George Whitworth's vision more elusive.

Nevertheless, during commencement in May 1990, Whitworth College will graduate its 10,000th undergraduate student. More than 8,000 of those students have received their degrees since 1955. More importantly, many of those graduates now live and work throughout the country and around the world, making a positive difference in their respective communities. For 100 years Whitworth faculty and adminstrators have sought to provide a quality liberal arts education in a supportive Christian environment. For 100 years this ideal has encouraged students to tackle tough ethical issues, to make important life style choices, and to develop a world view centered on service to humankind.

Among all those who reflect the Whitworth spirit is one to whom I wish to pay special tribute. Dayne Nix graduated from Whitworth in 1945, and in 1947 he began work in the business office, where he later became the bursar or treasurer. Forty-three years later, Dayne continues in that position. According to his co-workers, through the years Dayne has anonymously helped many students, providing from his own funds for the needs that arise.

This centennial year witnessed one other unique expression of thanks for the work of Whitworth faculty. An anonymous graduate from the college, known only as the "Mystery Man," contacted faculty who had spent more than twenty years at Whitworth and offered as many as seventeen professors and their spouses two-week vacations to anywhere in the world with all expenses paid. The story of the "Mystery Man" attracted journalistic attention literally all over the world and testified to the lasting impact of the Whitworth experience.

George Whitworth's vision has had many nurturers: Amos Fox, Donald MacKay, Ward Sullivan, Francis Hardwick, Frank Warren, Mark Koehler, Ed Lindaman, Bob Mounce, and now Art De Jong. But with all due respect to presidents and administrators who have led this college, the Whitworth dream has been best nurtured by faculty: David Guy, that all-around mathematician, athletic coach, campus surveyor, and tenor in the choir, and James Countermine, who gave his typewriter away to Grant Rodkey so he could go better-prepared to Harvard medical school. It has been the likes of Marion Jenkins, Gus Schlauch, Clem Simpson, Fenton Duvall, and Homer Cunningham who have given their heart and soul for their students; in recent years professors such as Harry Dixon, Leonard Oakland, Laura Bloxham, Pat Stien, Pat MacDonald, and Forrest Baird have represented that legacy of teaching excellence. The commitment to the education of mind and spirit continues to guide Whitworth into its second hundred years.

CHAIRMEN OF THE BOARD OF TRUSTEES

Rev. George F. Whitworth 1890-1901

George H. Stone 1901

Rev. A. L. Hutchison 1902-1905

Rev. A. H. Barnhisel 1906-1907

Rev. A. L. Hutchison 1907-1912

Rev. Murdock McLeod 1912-1914

Rev. Donald D. MacKay 1914-1917

Jay P. Graves..1917-1918

Charles E. Marr..1918-1921

Robert L. Edmiston 1921-1923

William L. McEachran 1923-1959

Albert K. Arend 1959-1971

Kenneth W. Myers..1971-1974

Richard Langford 1974-1977

Jack W. Hatch 1977-1988

William R. Yinger...1988-

PRESIDENTS OF WHITWORTH COLLEGE

Rev. Amos T. Fox, B.L., B.D. 1890

Rev. Calvin W. Stewart, D.D. 1890-1898

Rev. Robert Boyd, D.D. 1898-1899

Franklin B. Gault, Ph.D. 1899-1905

Rev. Barend H. Kroeze, A.M., D.D. 1905-1909

Rev. Donald D. MacKay, A.M., D.D. 1911-1917

Charles A. Barry, M.A. (Acting President) 1917-1918

Rev. B. Scott Bates, D.D. 1918

Rev. Arthur Y. Beatie, D.D. 1919-1920

Charles A. Barry, M.A. (Acting President) 1920-1921

Rev. Willard H. Robinson, Ph.D. 1921-1923

Rev. Walter A. Stevenson, D.D., Ph.D. 1923-1927

Rev. Orrin E. Tiffany, Ph.D. (Acting President) 1927-1929

Rev. Ward W. Sullivan, Ph.D. 1929-1938

Francis T. Hardwick, Ph.D. (Acting President) 1938-1940

Rev. Frank F. Warren, M.A., D.D., LL.D., Litt. D. 1940-1963

Rev. Mark L. Koehler, Th.M., D.D., LL.D. 1964-1969

Clarence J. Simpson, Ph.D. (Acting President) 1969-1970

Edward B. Lindaman, L.H.D., Sc.D., D.D. 1970-1980

Duncan S. Ferguson, Ph.D. (Acting President)..............................1980-1981

Rev. Robert H. Mounce, Th.M., Ph.D. 1981-1987

Joseph P.H. Black, Th.M., (Acting President)................................1987-1988

Rev. Arthur J. De Jong, Th.M., D.D., S.T.D. 1988-

STUDENT BODY PRESIDENTS

1904-05	Dosu Doseff
1905-06	No record
1906-07	Charles Rodman
1907-08	No record
1908-09	Richard C. Doud
1909-10	No record
1910-11	Sidney Whitworth
1911-12	Augustus Williams
1912-13	Samuel A. Hoke
1913-14	Augustus Williams
1914-15	Ruth Lee
1915-16	Thomas R. Gunn
1916-17	No record
1917-18	Carl E. Clark
1918-19	College closed
1919-20	G. Carl Weller
1920-21	No record
1921-22	E. Miriam Cassill
1922-23	Owen C. Ennis
1923-24	Frank B. Henry
	Genevieve Welch
1924-25	Frank B. Henry
1925-26	Lawrence J. Mitchell
	Donald Beal
1926-27	Carl Laudenbach
1927-28	Karl K. Rupp
1928-29	Lewis G. Randall
1929-30	Everell R. Sharnbroich
1930-31	Forrest C. Travaille
1931-32	Loris Winn
1932-33	Owen J. Picton
1933-34	Ward N. Fancher, Jr.
1934-35	Keith A. Murray
1935-36	Daniel B. Fleming
1936-37	Charles H. Frazier
1937-38	Burton Alvis
1938-39	Garth A. Steele
1939-40	Eugene W. Muench
1940-41	Dougald Robinson
1941-42	Earl Klein
1942-43	Sam Smith
1943-44	Merle E. Wood
1944-45	Richard C. Schwab
1945-46	George R. Hendrick
1946-47	Odin A. Baugh
1947-48	Leonard A. Watson
1948-49	Gerald H. Mahaffey
1949-50	James W. Hardie
1950-51	Robert N. Davis
1951-52	Paul R. Schilperoort
1952-53	William J. Tatum
1953-54	Richard G. Gray
1954-55	David E. Crossley
1955-56	Michael D. Anderson

1956-57	Spencer W. Marsh
1957-58	Robert A. Gray
1958-59	Jack V. Rozell
1959-60	William D. Slemko
1960-61	C. Gary Tewinkel
1961-62	Ronald J. Van Der Werff
1962-63	Bennet Lindstrom
1963-64	Terry D. Casteel
1964-65	William E. Duvall
1965-66	M. Bruce McCullough
1966-67	Jon D. Freeberg
1967-68	Gary A. Tuttle
1968-69	Kent W. Jones
1969-70	David G. Lee
1970-71	Glen E. Hiemstra
1971-72	Robert J. Yinger
1972-73	Ronald B. Leighton
1973-74	Kim R. Hunter
1974-75	Jeffrey E. Hanson
1975-76	Craig A. Grant
1976-77	James J. Glower
1977-78	Daniel M. Thieme
1978-79	Bruce R. Hafferkamp
1979-80	Steven M. Lowe
1980-81	Douglas A. Nave
1981-82	Michael D. Wendlandt
1982-83	Linda J. Gillingham
1983-84	Dale K. Edwards
1984-85	Marquis I. Nuby
1985-86	Brad P. Larkin
1986-87	James B. "J.B." Meade
1987-88	James B. "J.B." Meade
1988-89	Eric R. Roecks
1989-90	David J. Harris

TUITION

1890	$ 24
1900	$ 50
1910	$ 60
1920	$ 80
1930	$ 120
1940	$ 150
1950	$ 300
1960	$ 580
1970	$ 750
1980	$ 3,950
1990	$ 9,500

UNDERGRADUATE ENROLLMENT

1890	15
1901	23
1910	63
1915	80
1920	98
1928	55
1930	105
1935	200
1940	223
1945	374
1950	755
1955	837
1960	877
1965	1147
1970	940
1975	1274
1980	1225
1985	1231
1989	1237

ALUMNI IDEALS AWARDS

Awarded each year to a graduating senior for outstanding abilities in academic and extracurricular activities.

1939	Mary Trevitt	1963	Janet L. Maring
1940	Mary E. Koper	1964	Michal A. Koehler
1941	Dorsey Bailey	1965	Robert G. Sharp
1942	Lee Rodkey	1966	M. Bruce McCullough
1943	Sam Smith	1968	Joan E. Quall
1944	Eleanor Hook	1969	Laura Bloxham
1945	Marjorie M. Klein	1971	Glen Hiemstra
1946	E. Louise Klebe		Cinda Warner
1947	Odin A. Baugh	1975	James Patten
1948	Mary L. Taylor	1976	Helen Tait
	Helmuth Bekowies		Craig Grant
1949	Betty L. Lange	1977	Robyn Ramer
1950	Lois McConnell		David Vaughn
1951	Carol Gray Anderson	1978	Patricia Campbell
	Robert L. Bruce	1979	Robert Dykstra
1952	David G. Beamer		Susan Lonborg
1953	Elizabeth Muir Olds	1980	Susan Schilperoort
1954	Jack W. Bishop	1981	Steve Benson
	Richard G. Gray		Jim Craig
1955	Joseph M. Tewinkel, Jr.		Richard Yramategui
	Helen L. Greiner	1982	Mike Charles
1956	Michael D. Anderson	1983	Beth Kehle
1957	Joanne E. Orr	1984	Randie K. Fong
1958	Robert A. Gray		Dennis F. Salisbury
1959	Harland L. Gilliland	1985	Marquis Nuby
1960	Janet E. Anderson	1986	Jill Gill
1961	Ronald C. Turner	1987	Kenneth D. Urie
1962	Kathleen F. Goode	1988	James "J.B." Meade
	Rodney E. Espey	1989	Michael K. LeRoy

ALUMNI DISTINGUISHED SERVICE AWARD WINNERS

The award is given to an alumnus of the year for outstanding qualities of leadership in service to the community, his/her alma mater, and to society in general.

1963	Dorothy Farr Dixon	1980	Mark L. Koehler
1964	Karl K. Rupp	1981	R. Kay Brown
1965	George Rossman	1983	Rev. Andy Jarvis
	Marion Jenkins	1985	Paul Merkel
1966	Estella E. Baldwin	1986	Arthur E. Symons, Jr.
1967	Dr. Keith A. Murray	1988	Bruce D. Finlayson
1968	Dr. William C. Richter		
1969	Dorothea Teeter		
1972	Dennis Ashlock		
1975	Stanley Gwinn		
1976	Richard Hanks		
1978	Dorothy McLarren		
1979	David A. Morley		
	Mina Spalding		

INDEX

SUBJECT INDEX

The index of subjects is limited to the general areas of student life covered in the text